CRAFT YOUR SOUND

FIRST REVISED EDITION

GIRISH PATRO

PARTRIDGE

To order additional copies of this book, contact
Partridge India
000 800 919 0634 (Call Free)
+91 000 80091 90634 (Outside India)
orders.india@partridgepublishing.com

www.partridgepublishing.com/india

Dedicated to my Mentors, Students and my Family

CONTENTS

PREFACE

We must agree that the role of Arts, Commerce & Science are equally important in Career Development to survive, but we have lost the focus on 'Arts' or 'Skills' in our Education System which used to be our Assets. The goals to write this book are,

1. To develop and make a full-time career in Performing Arts and Skills in Audio Production and Sound Reinforcement and also motivate to manufacture Audio Electronic Products: The lessons describes the procedures and methods to develop a set of Skills and motivates the reader to become a self-trainable content creator, a performer, a service provider or an Audio Electronic Products' Manufacturer. The lessons describe to learn responsibilities and motivates to find too many solutions for each problem and applying one of them according to the demand

2. To spread awareness about right informations regarding Audio Production and Sound Reinforcement processes to the listeners, consumers, music lovers: Learning awareness about Career Opportunities, Practical Applications, Work Spaces, Team Members and their Responsibilities …etc are very much essential which are simplified and properly organised in the lessons. If we put an analogy of learning all about our audio industry with human body analysis, then the first lesson would be showing you a human body instead of explaining a human intestine.

3. To establish and maintain a long term business environment in Audio Industry: The lessons always motivate and encourage the reader to maintain transparency by monitoring and removing dirty politics and other related loopholes existing in Audio Industry through demanding and mentioning terms and responsibilities clearly in contract agreements.

The author may put some analogy to explain each lesson such as 'Cooking Techniques' as 'Sound Mixing Techniques'; 'Hot' as 'Loud', where hot can be a touch or taste sensation and loud (loudness or volume control in your remote or a dedicated knob in your playback system) as a listening sensation. If we put an analogy of learning audio recording skills with riding a bike, then the author love to explain the bike riding skills, maintenance of a bike, introducing recent technology used, safety precautions for the biker, traffic rules and regulations, but the author hasn't explained the features and functions of different products (different brands of bikes), because features and functions changes according to recent technology development. And features and functions of different products (different brands of bikes) can be learnt through their respective official websites so that the learner as a customer will make his / her own decision about purchasing a product (certain brand of a bike) as per his / her requirements.

In this book the author may have mentioned few products as examples to focus on the Technology applied in the products; that doesn't mean he promote those products. We can't rely on technology to correct major amount of errors because it has some limitations. For a limited time period, the technology can be used to correct a minimum amount of errors. It is better to use technology in methods for practicing more of the arts or skills so that a major amount of error will be reduced at the input.

ABOUT THE AUTHOR

Girish Patro, is an accomplished Music Production Engineer and a well known Trainer in Sound Engineering and Music Production.

He is the elder son of Gosto Chandra Patro(Carnatic Music Trainer for Singers and Musicians, Music Therapist and Ayurvedacharya) and Sujata Patro(Ghazal Lyricist) and also grandson of Late Bhakta Bachhala Patro (Music Therapist, Aroma Therapist, Ayurvedacharya, All India Radio Veena Player at Cuttack).

Since childhood, he has a passion for music performing on stage. He is a trained Tabla Player under the guidance of Raghunath Patro(Music Arranger at All India Radio Jeypore).For around 22 years, he did practice playing Tabla for 6 hours every day in the evening. He owns 7 years Diploma in performing Tabla from Odisha Sangeet Natak Akademi, Bhubaneswar.

When he was studying engineering in Electronics and Instrumentation Branch at Centurion University, the evolution of audio technology intrigued him which further guided him to get a certification from Apple as an authorised Logic Pro 9 user in 2013 and successfully completed Music Production Engineering and Sound Design training program at Audiomedia, Chennai.

In 2013, he won Crowdsourcing Week's Music Sore Competition which is his first achievement on an international platform. For more details please visit

https://crowdsourcingweek.com/blog/crowdsourcing-weeks-official-music-score-competition-announces-winner/

He invested his money, earned from Crowdsourcing Week's Music Sore Competition, to learn Sound Engineering. In 2014, he got a diploma in Sound Engineering & Sound Recording from Sound Engineering Academy, Trivandrum.

He is mentored by Mr. T.Selvakumar(Director at Audiomedia, Author of Sample Libraries at Yamaha, Authorised distributor of AMS Neve products), Mr. Didier Weiss(Acoustician, FOH Mix Engineer), Mr. Bobby Baskaran(Music Producer, Melbourne), Mr. Stephen Webber(Record Producer, New York), Mr. K T Fransis(FOH Mix Engineer for A R Rahman), Late John Anthony(Electric Guitarist for A R Rahman), Late K S Ravi(Retired Sound Engineer at Doordarshan, Mumbai), Mr. Deepak Sugathan(Former Instructor at Audiomedia and KMMC).

He worked as a Sound Engineer Assistant for the Music Producer Mr. Ram Sampath at Omgrown Music Studio Mumbai who provide Music Production services to Ad Film Industry and Indian Cinema Industry. His work and workflow of each assigned task are appreciated by Music Performers, Record Producers and Indian Cinema Producers.

He has a unique skills of Music Programming for lead acoustic instruments that sounds very natural. He has a keen sense and observation of Audio Post-production skills that fulfil international standard requirements.

He has started creating Indian Musical Instrument Library for Audio Content Creators. For more details, please visit
https://www.pianobook.co.uk/author/girishpatro/

He has trained many more sound engineers, music performers, music educators at "Sound Engineering Academy" Trivandrum and "Centurion University" Bhubaneswar, who are currently working at the Music Industry in India and abroad and published books about Sound Engineering, Music Production and Music Business.

He found that most of the people in India and other Asian Countries are not aware of many informations regarding Career Opportunities in Audio Industry. Most of the budding sound engineers and music performers are deviated their responsibilities from "focusing on crafting and creating rich contents" to "focusing more on technical enhancement of poor contents or average quality of contents in their audio-visual products".Thus he has decided to write and publish books which include valuable informations, industry standard workflow procedures and methods to develop a set of skills used in Audio Production so that each reader will become a self-trainable content creator, performer, educator or a service provider.

This book is dedicated to budding sound engineers, music performers, music educators, musical content creators, film and music lovers.

Now, he is looking for sharing his work experiences and nurture the skills of potential candidates (music performers and budding sound engineers) and would love to release his own Indian Musical Instrument Library and Original Music Compositions.

For more details about the author, pre-order other upcoming books, Please visit

https://www.linkedin.com/in/girishpatro/

https://balancedsoundscape.wixsite.com/girishpatro/

CHAPTER 1

INTRODUCTION TO AUDIO PRODUCTION

Objectives:

To learn and understand

1. Listening Environment
2. Observational Skill (Listening Skill) Development
3. Difference between Rich Contents & Poor Contents
4. Rich Contents' Development
5. Different Methods of Analysing each Sound

CHAPTER 1.1

PRACTICAL APPLICATIONS

Acoustic Treatment:

a) Indoor Area - Acoustic Treatment of Class rooms, Home, Corporate Office, Meeting Hall, Cinema Hall, Mall, Studio for recording, mixing, mastering, dubbing.

b) Noise Control at working area such as Live Concerts, Civil Construction Projects, Traffic Control Area, Machinery Lab during Production.

Audio Product Manufacturing:

a) *Audio Production for Software Applications*
    Gaming applications, Audio Applications, Audio-visual Applications

b) *Audio Production for Sound Libraries*
    Audio Loop libraries, Musical Instrument Libraries, Foley Sound Libraries, Sound Effect Libraries, Sound Libraries for DJ shows, Radio Broadcasting and many more

Role of Quality Check Department for Professional and Consumer Audio Product Manufacturing for hardwares:

Each product that produce sound, maintain the following parameters

a) Loudness Control (Below Threshold Level) of the audio devices (e.g. speakers, monitors, earphones, headphones) and other devices that produce sound (e.g:- vacuum cleaner, Motor bikes).
b) Frequency Response Characteristics of audio devices (e.g. Microphones).

Audio Production and Audio Broadcasting: (using Professional Audio Equipments)

From Audio Pre-production to Audio Post-production we do record, edit, mix, master the tracks.

a) Audio Recording - During recording, Critical listening concept is useful for Microphone Selection, Mic Placement and Selection of the Location for Recording.
b) Audio Mixing - While Mixing audio tracks, we do analyse the frequency response of each instrument and we also control the dynamics of the tracks. It means the critical listening concept plays an important role during mixing. We also apply the theory of critical listening to use audio equipments such as Mixing Consoles, Signal Processing Units…etc for mixing.
c) Audio Mastering - If you are an expert on critical listening then only you can identify the issues in the audio track. If you are mastering a music album then the sound texture of each audio track's output should be same. After mastering the audio track, each element(e.g. Kick, Bass) of the song should be identified by the listener during playback on all type of output devices including mobile phone speakers.

Forensic Report Preparation of provided audio by Crime Branch:

Each material and each space are having a certain kind of resonating frequency.

a) Resonating Frequency - A frequency at which the material will resonate (Vibrate with maximum amplitude).
b) Role of Resonating Frequency is to study the environment of the audio provided.

While preparing a forensic report we do identify the sound sources using Limiter, Spectrum Analyser Hardware units, Artificial Intelligence and prepare a case study report and submit it to the Crime Branch Department.

Pest Control:

a) Mosquito Repellent Devices, Firmware Applications are used to get rid of mosquitoes and insects.
b) Some devices are used in farm house gardens which produce ultra high frequency to attract honey bees for Honey Production.

Medical Applications:

a) *Healing Techniques using Vibro-acoustic Therapy*
   A sports-man hurts many times during practice session every-day. To get relief from that pain the physiotherapist diagnose the patient and note down the parameters such as density and resonating frequency of the muscles. In this case, dedicated speakers are used to produce that resonating frequency of the muscle (low frequencies) that heals the muscular pain with in few minutes.

b) *Healing Techniques using Music Therapy*

    It is a time consuming process than Aroma Therapy but very much effective. Almost all diseases can be healed by Music therapy; few of them are mentioned in the book "About Music Industry for Beginners".

Agricultural Department:

a) Role of Music for Growth of grains, Leaves, Roots of trees and plants
b) Growth of quantity and quality of milk of Cows, Buffaloes, Goats...etc

CHAPTER 1.2

BASIC FUNDAMENTALS OF PHYSICS

1.2.1. Sound Sources:

A Sound Source is of two types -

a) **Point Source** - It is an infinitely small device which radiates sound spherically from one point in space. If we apply 1 watt of electrical power to a point source, it will produce 1 watt of acoustical power with 100% efficiency. Energy radiated from a point source travels equally all directions.

Inverse Square Law says, "When the radius of the elliptical wavefront from a point source is doubled, the surface area will increase to 4 times and the sound pressure level will drop by 6 decibel."

b) **Line Source** - It is an infinitely line source which radiate sound cylindrically from a line in space. The infinite line source emits a wave that is approximately cylindrical in shape. Since the diverging wave is not expanding in two dimensions, the sound pressure level change with increasing distance is half that of the point source. The sound pressure level from an ideal line source will decrease at 3 dB per distance doubling rather than 6 dB.When the radius of the cylindrical wave front from the line source is doubled, the surface area will increase to twice and there will a decrease in sound pressure level of 3 dB.

Inverse Square Law also says, "When the radius of a cylindrical wavefront from a line source is doubled, the surface area will increase to 2 times and the sound pressure level will drop by 3 dB." It means a line source sounds much louder than a point source.

(Point Source)   (Line Source)

If you put an analogy of Point Source and Line Source visually, then an electric bulb is point source where as a tube light is a line source. During electric bulb decoration on the ceiling for festivals and marriage functions in India, each electric bulb (a point source) is arranged in such a way that the combination of electric bulbs forms a line to produce more intensity of light and to both left and right side you can find tube lights hanging on the bamboo poles.

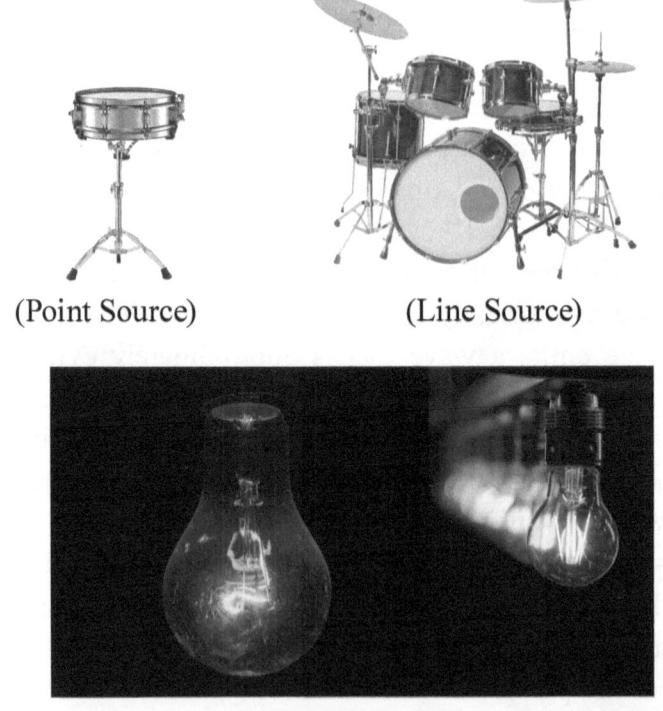

(Point Source)   (Line Source)

Point Source	Line Source
Lead Vocal	Backing Vocals
One of the element of a Drum Kit such as Snare, Kick or Tom	Drum Kit
Any Brass Instrument such as Saxophone, Tuba or French Horn	Brass Ensemble
Any Woodwind Instrument such as Piccolo, Flute, Oboe, Clarinet or Bassoon	Woodwind Ensemble
Any String Instrument such as Violin, Cello, Viola, or Double Bass	String Ensemble
Any Percussion Instrument such as Concert Bass Drum, Darbuka, Djembe, Timpani, Chenda, Kanjira or Udu	Percussion Ensemble

During a concert, a point source (the lead singer, a lead instrument player) is always placed at the front of the stage where as a line source (a brass ensemble section, a woodwind ensemble section, a string ensemble section, a drummer who plays a drum kit, a pianist who plays a piano, backing vocals), that sounds louder than the point sources, are placed behind the point sources at the middle of the stage, backend of the stage, left corner of the stage or right corner of the stage because when the sound of each sound source reaches to the audience (listeners), collectively they sound evenly (equally) because the loud sound from line sources travels longer distance (results less dynamics), that diffuse in the air and also reflect more (more reflected sound) than the soft sound of the point sources to reach the audience (listeners).

If a line source and a point source are placed at the front of the stage and if you are not using any sound reinforcement system, then the line source sounds much louder than a point source (6dB drop of a point source at a particular distance versus 3dB drop of a line source at that particular distance) during delivering musical sounds by the music performers at the same time.

A line source sounds much louder than a point source. Therefore a line source must not placed near by the point source, else the sound of point source won't be audible. This effect is called as "Masking" of a line source over the point source. During Jamming Session of musicians and singers, the point source always need a sound reinforcement system to amplify its sound where as the line source won't need a sound reinforcement system.

A line source always placed behind a point source because a line source, (multiple point sources arranged in a line) provide more intensity or loudness than a point source.

Homework:

Identify the point sources, line sources and their placements, when you are watching a music band, a symphony orchestra or any musical show to prepare a report for your reference that help you learn the upcoming chapters faster.

1.2.2. Types of a Vibration of Sound Sources:

A vibration is of two types:

a) *Free Vibration* - If a material vibrates by itself at its own frequency (called as natural frequency), then the vibration is called free vibration.

b) *Forced Vibration* - If a material vibrates by applying a force, then the vibration is called forced vibration. When we apply a force on a string of a guitar instrument, the string vibrates. When the force is removed from the string, the loudness of the sound gradually decreases (fade out).The intensity of sound at which it is maximum in the forced vibration, is known as Resonance. The frequency at which resonance occurs is called as Resonating Frequency.

1.2.3. The Medium:

A Medium is of 3 types -

a) *Solid Medium*: Sound travels faster but lesser distance in the solid medium as compared to liquid medium and gaseous medium because the molecules are closely packed. To make the sound travel in a solid medium up to a longer distance, you need to invest more energy as compared to liquid medium and gaseous medium. We use audio amplifiers to make travel the sound to a larger distance through audio cables.

b) *Liquid Medium*: Sound travels slower but more distance in the liquid medium as compared to solid medium because the molecules are loosely packed (having an elastic property).To make the sound travel in a liquid medium, you need to invest less energy as compared to solid medium and more energy need to be invested as compared to gaseous medium.

Sound travels faster but lesser distance in the liquid medium as compared to gaseous medium because the molecules are closely packed as compared to gaseous medium.

c) **Gaseous Medium:** Sound travels slower but more distance in the gaseous medium as compared to liquid medium and solid medium because the molecules are loosely packed, providing an elastic property. To make the sound travel in a gaseous medium, you need to invest less energy as compared to liquid medium and solid medium. We use acoustically treated and acoustically designed amphitheatres to make travel the sound to a larger distance through air medium.

1.2.3.1. *Sound Propagation in the Air Medium:*

The bass sound travels omni-directionally i.e, equal distance to all directions from the sound source. If there are multiple number of barriers to stop the sound, the bass sound (low frequency) travels slowly upto a larger distance as compared to mid frequency range and high frequency range. Low frequency can't be absorbed so easily. To control low frequencies we use Bass Traps at the corner of indoor areas and phase cancellation techniques by placing other speakers with distance and delay measurements properly near the residential areas and play back the inverted (180 degree out of phase) low frequency sound on those speakers against the low frequency produced by FOH (Front of House) speakers to cancel the bass sound near the residential areas at the outdoor location.

Mid frequency travels quicker than low frequency and travels a bit more directional (elliptical in shape) than low frequency if there is no barrier to stop or diverge its direction.

Mid frequency can be reflected, diverged, diffused and absorbed through a proper acoustic treatment.

The treble sound source travels quicker than mid frequencies and much more directional than mid frequency sound by shifting more energy from the sides to front and back if there are no barriers to stop the sound. High frequency can be absorbed, diverged or reflected very easily than mid frequencies because it travels like an arrow or a bullet.

If the power supplied to sound sources of each frequency range is same, then the travel of each audible frequency ranges (low, mid, high) in the air medium without any barrier(outdoor locations) and with multiple barriers(acoustically treated indoor areas) are shown in the two diagrams below.

1. ***Sound Propagation of types of sound sources in the air of a free-field area*** *(outdoor area)*:

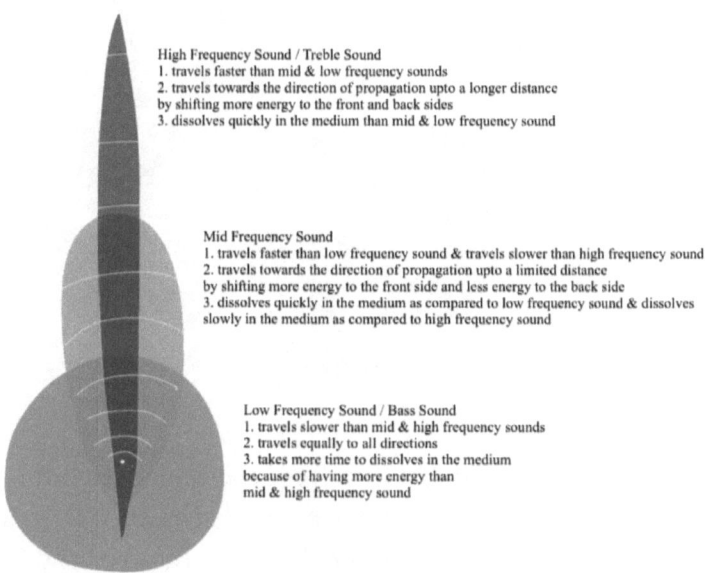

High Frequency Sound / Treble Sound
1. travels faster than mid & low frequency sounds
2. travels towards the direction of propagation upto a longer distance by shifting more energy to the front and back sides
3. dissolves quickly in the medium than mid & low frequency sound

Mid Frequency Sound
1. travels faster than low frequency sound & travels slower than high frequency sound
2. travels towards the direction of propagation upto a limited distance by shifting more energy to the front side and less energy to the back side
3. dissolves quickly in the medium as compared to low frequency sound & dissolves slowly in the medium as compared to high frequency sound

Low Frequency Sound / Bass Sound
1. travels slower than mid & high frequency sounds
2. travels equally to all directions
3. takes more time to dissolves in the medium because of having more energy than mid & high frequency sound

The bass (low frequency) sound travels omni-directionally i.e, equal distance to all directions from the sound source. The treble (high frequency) sound travels much more directional than bass sound by shifting more energy from the sides to front and back. The treble (high frequency) sound travels faster to a longer distance in a free field (without any barrier) and disappears faster than bass (low frequency) sound in each medium. Here 'disappear faster' means diffuse faster by converting sound energy into heat energy because of friction among the air molecules by the force applied through a sound source having potential energy or kinetic energy and absorption of that heat energy. The diagram from the top view of Sound Propagation of types of sound sources in air of a free-field is shown above.

2. ***Sound Propagation of types of sound sources in the air of an acoustically treated room*** *(indoor area):*

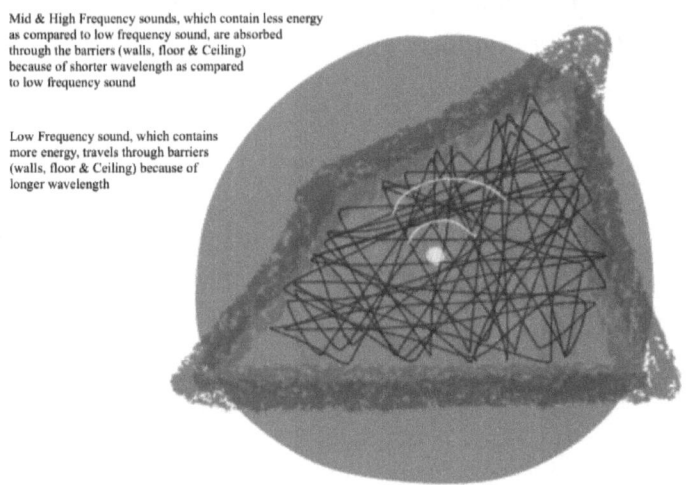

Mid & High Frequency sounds, which contain less energy as compared to low frequency sound, are absorbed through the barriers (walls, floor & Ceiling) because of shorter wavelength as compared to low frequency sound

Low Frequency sound, which contains more energy, travels through barriers (walls, floor & Ceiling) because of longer wavelength

In the diagram above, the mid frequencies and high frequencies can be easily controlled or easily converted into heat energy and absorbed using acoustical treatment but it is not very easy to control low frequency because it has more power, travels slowly. Because of conversion of sound energy into heat energy and absorption of heat energy, the mid frequencies and high frequencies can be kept inside an acoustical treated room but the low frequency travels through the isolated solid barriers(walls, floor, ceiling).When a Disc Jockey performs live in a concert venue, the people inside their home nearby residential areas and outside that concert venue can feel more low frequencies than mid frequencies and high frequencies.

The diagram from the top view of Sound Propagation of types of sound sources in air of an acoustically treated room is shown below.

Effect of change in Air Temperature on Density of Air Medium during Sound Propagation:

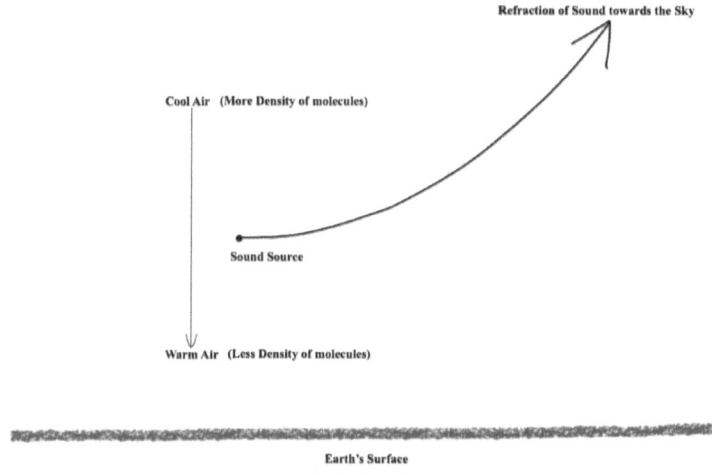

During the night time after sunset, when the upper layer of the air medium becomes cooler (having less temperature and more air density) than lower layer near the earth's surface, then the sound from the sound source nearby the earth's surface refract or diverge the sound towards the sky as shown in the diagram above.

During sunset, when the temperature or density of lower layer of the air medium nearby the earth's surface becomes similar to the temperature or density of the upper layer of the air medium then the sound nearby the earth's surface won't refract or diverge the sound towards the sky or towards the earth surface but travels parallel to the earth's surface. It means the upper and lower layers of air medium are having almost similar properties (air densities and temperatures of upper and lower layers of air medium are almost same).

During day time after sunrise, the upper layer of the air medium becoming warm (having more temperature and less air density) due to incident rays of sun light and the lower layer of the air medium nearby the earth's surface became cool already (having less temperature and more air density) during the mid night. So the sound nearby the earth's surface refract or diverge the sound towards the earth surface.

It means the sound travels through a parabolic path just like the way gravitational force act on a cricket ball thrown from the boundary to the wicket keeper as shown in the diagram below.

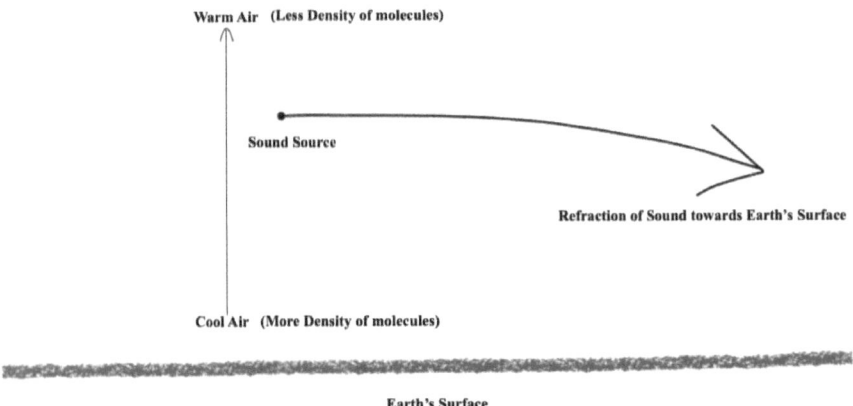

Note: The temperature of the air medium is inversely proportional to the density of the air medium

Sound Wave in Air Medium:

When we apply a force on a material, it vibrates and sets into motion of nearby molecules in the air medium. The molecules passes their energy to the nearby molecules and start a reaction, called a Sinusoidal Wave (sine wave).Due to elastic property of air medium, the vibrating material move outwards which compress the molecules close to it, resulting an increase in air pressure of the compressed molecules. When the vibrating material move inwards, it creates rarefaction, resulting decrease in air pressure. During vibration, the molecules don't advance with the wave, but they vibrate with respect to a common point and thus the sound travels from one place to other until it's energy getting converted into heat.

1.2.4. Components of a Sound Wave: (P-H-F-W-A-V-E)

Phase: Two sound waves or more than two sound waves traveling together may be in-phase or out of phase. If two signals are in-phase (zero degree out of phase), then when you sum those two signals the loudness has to be doubled or increased. If two signals are out of phase, then when you sum those two signals the loudness will be reduced or decreased. Phase issues can be divided into two parts.

Absolute Phase Issue - If an audio signal is out of phase by 180 degree to the other audio signal (reference original signal) having identical loudness, then the sum of these two signals provide zero output. It means, the signals are fully cancelled to each other and you won't hear any sound when those two signals are summed.

If these audio signals have non identical loudness and 180 degree out of phase to each other, then the loudness of sum of these two signals provide less audible sound compared to the loudness of individual sound of each audio signal.

Relative Phase Issue - If an audio signal is delayed by a certain time period in milli seconds to the reference original signal(1 degree to 179 degree out of phase), then

a) the fundamental frequency of that original signal and its overtones at low frequency ranges vanishes and the sum of these two signal provide a brighter sound with less loudness.

b) the fundamental frequency of that original signal and its overtones at upper mid frequency ranges vanishes and the sum of these two signal provide a hollow sound with less loudness. e.g:- certain point source based musical instrument can't be noticeable during playback.

Phase correction is one of the important process for time correction and waveform alignment during sound editing.

Harmonics:It is the multiple of fundamental frequency of a sound source. A sound produces fundamental frequency (called as first harmonics) with a series of secondary or sympathetic vibrations at a regular interval of fundamental frequency (called as harmonics).Fundamental frequency, taken as reference, is one of the resonating frequencies. The resonating frequencies of an instrument vary according to the energy applied at different positions of the instrument to generate an audible sound. Harmonics is of two types. The even integer multiple of fundamental frequency is called as second order harmonics or even harmonics(e.g.:- 200Hz, 400Hz, 800Hz…etc.).The odd integer multiple of fundamental frequency is called as third order harmonics or odd harmonics (e.g.:- 100Hz, 300Hz, 500Hz…etc.).Most non-linear loads produce odd harmonics. A square wave contains only odd (3rd) harmonics only whereas a triangular wave contains even (2nd) harmonics. A sine wave doesn't contain any harmonics.

Tube and Analog Tape Distortion (Saturation) takes away the transient sound (less sustained sound that exist for less time period such as a fraction of a second) that our ear never notice but notice the sustained tones because Tube and Analog Tape Distortion introduce Even Harmonics (e.g.:- 200Hz, 400Hz, 800Hz…etc.).Tube and Analog Tape Distortion sounds rounder and smoother (smoother as per visual perception - a Velvet Cloth material feels smoother if you touch the cloth material).Products belong to Neve, Harrison companies provide even harmonics distortions. Blues, Jazz, Classical music (slower tempo based songs) contain more sustained instruments that prefer more signal processing of even harmonics distortion.

Transistors always introduce odd harmonics (e.g.:- 100Hz, 300Hz, 500Hz…etc.).Transistor sounds buzzier (grainy as per visual perception - a premium Raymond Cloth Material feels grainy if you touch the cloth material).Mid frequencies and high frequencies (treble sound) can be easily manipulated to make it sound grainy, upfront, prominent, audible, identifiable by using transistor and transistor-diode based audio equipments. Products belong to SSL, API companies provides odd harmonics distortions. Pop, Rock Music (medium to higher tempo based songs) contain less sustained instruments (transient instruments) that prefer more signal processing of odd harmonics distortion.

Frequency: It is the reciprocal of time-period(1/T).It is the number of vibrations (oscillations) per one second; it is also the number of cycles per second. The faster vibration gives the higher pitch, the slower vibration gives the lower pitch. It is perceived as pitch and measured in Hertz.

The low frequency in the audible frequency range contributes power (energy) to the sound. More low frequencies gives boominess and muddiness problems of the bass sound. The mid frequency in the audible frequency range contributes presence to the sound through which the sound source feels nearer to the listener. More mid frequencies feels distorted and noisy for human ears. The high frequency in the audible frequency range contributes clarity. More high frequencies results hissness problems of the treble sound. The music played with low pass filter used to be ignored where as music with full range of frequencies grabs more attention of the listeners for up to 3 minutes.

The human listening range of frequency is from 20 Hertz (20Hz) to 20000 Hertz (20 Kilo Hertz or 20KHz).The 20 Hertz (20 cycles per one second or 20 vibrations (oscillations) per one second) is perceived as lower pitch and it contains longer wavelength. The 20 Kilo Hertz (20000 cycles, 20000 vibrations or oscillations per one second) is perceived as higher pitch and it contains smaller wavelength.

Frequency response of human ear is not equally sensitive to each audible frequency from 20Hz to 20KHz. At a lower sound pressure level (having less amplitude), the low frequencies and high frequencies can't be noticed properly. But we can notice mid frequencies because sensitivity of human ear is great at 1KHz and above, and human ear's sensitivity is the best at 2KHz to 4KHz. At higher level, we can hear all the audible frequencies.

A human being can feel the change in loudness of mid frequency range, if the loudness of mid frequency range is changed(increased or decreased) by 3dB.A human being can feel the change in loudness of low frequency range, if the loudness of low frequency range is changed(increased or decreased) by 10dB. A human being can feel the change in loudness of high frequency range, if the loudness of high frequency range is changed (increased or decreased) by 4.5dB to 6 dB depends on his/her age.

As our age increases, the thickness of our eardrum increases and size of pinna increases, which means mass of the ear drum increases and captures more sound as more sound waves incident on larger pinna size. If thickness of our eardrum increases, the number of vibrations of our eardrum decreases and become less sensitive towards high frequencies but become more sensitive towards low frequencies. So, older people can't hear more than 12KHz treble sound where as young adults can hear upto 17.5KHz treble sound and because of thinner eardrum and smaller size of pinna, kids can hear upto 20KHz treble sound clearly. Similarly, because of thicker eardrum and larger pinna size, the older people can hear 20Hz bass sound onwards clearly where as young adults can hear from 30Hz bass sound onwards and kids can hear from 90Hz bass sound onwards. Therefore, as our age increases, the audible frequency range decreases or shifts from 90Hz - 20KHz range to 20Hz - 12KHz range of frequencies.

Note: To make the sound of background music or supporting instruments (such as background choir) feel like coming from a larger distance, we cut the mid frequency range using a band-stop filter. We use this technique for a stereo minus track(karaoke track) to create a space for a lead vocal during recording session.

When two louder tones, separated by less than about 50 Hz, summed together, results regular rise and falls of the loudness of the sound, called as 'beat' of the sound. If the difference of those two louder tones increases to more than 50Hz, the beat changes to an additional difference of tone. If the difference of those two louder tones increases beyond a semitone, the combined sound gradually disappears.

Wavelength: It is the distance travelled through a complete cycle. It is also the distance travelled through two zero-crossing points of a wave. Wavelengths of the audible frequencies(20Hz to 20KHz) in air, range from about 17 meter to 17 milli meter. Wavelength of 1 kHz in air is around 0.334 m (1.13 foot).

Amplitude: It is the height (upto the crest) or depth (upto the trough) of each half cycle of a sound wave. It is also the distance from the initial state of the material travelled after applying a force to the material due to vibration with respect to a common point. It is perceived as loudness and measured in decibels. The threshold of hearing for a human being is 0 decibel (0 dB).The threshold of pain (threshold of feeling) for a human being is 120 decibel (120 dB).

When the sound from two neighbouring instruments contains similar tones at different loudness level, the louder tone may completely mask the softer one. It may change the character of the quieter sound(masked sound) that need to be strengthen or to increase the apparent spatial separation. Note that loud harmonics of the louder sound can also cause masking to the soft sound.

Velocity: It is a speed of sound with direction through air medium. Speed is the distance per unit time. Humidity and temperature can affect the speed of sound.

Envelope: It refers to change in loudness over time. It is the variation of amplitude with respect to time. It has four stages - Attack, Decay, Sustain, Release.

Attack is the initial stage of an envelope to make the sound travel through air medium. On attack stage, the adjacent molecules to the sound source vibrates rapidly and increase the amplitude or loudness of the sound because of getting more energy from the sound source. The time taken to reach the maximum of the loudness (peak of the amplitude) of the sound and complete the attack stage, is called as attack time.

Decay is the second stage of an envelope. On decay stage, the molecules begins to loose its energy (amplitude or loudness of the sound).The time taken to loose or decay the maximum of the loudness (peak of the amplitude) of the sound and complete the decay stage, is called as decay time.

Sustain is the third stage of an envelope. On sustain stage, the energy of the molecules remain constant (constant amplitude or constant loudness of the sound).The time taken to remain constant energy of the vibration of the molecules and complete the sustain stage, is called as sustain time.

Release is the fourth stage or final stage of an envelope. On release stage, the energy (amplitude or loudness of the sound) of the molecules diffuse or disappear in the air medium because of absorption of remaining energy of the vibrating molecules on this last stage by the air medium.

Envelope of a sound wave also can be generally divided into 2 stages - Attack and Release. The attack depends on the type of frequency. If the sound source produce low frequency, the envelope contains more attack time (slower attack or longer attack) due to its larger wavelength. If the sound source produce high frequency, the envelope contains less attack time (faster attack or shorter attack) due to its smaller wavelength. The release depends on the sustain of the sound source. For more sustained instruments or more sustained sound source, the envelope contains more release time(slower release or longer release).For less sustained instruments (transient instruments) or less sustained sound source, the envelope contains less release time(faster release or shorter release).

Envelope of a Sustained Low Frequency Sound Source:

A floor-tom from the drum kit, one of the sides that produce bass sound of a pakhawaj or a bass guitar contains low frequencies and more sustain which means it contains more attack time (slower attack or longer attack) and more release time (slower release or longer release).

Envelope of a transient Low Frequency Sound Source:

A kick from the drum kit or one of the sides that produce bass sound of a thavil contains low frequencies and less sustain which means it contains more attack time (slower attack or longer attack) and less release time (faster release or shorter release).

Envelope of a Sustained Mid Frequency Sound Source:

A dholak, naal, tabla, a mridangam, a maddale or a kanjira has mid frequencies and more sustain which means it contains medium or average (neither more nor less) attack time (moderate attack) and more release time (slower release or longer release).

Envelope of a transient Mid Frequency Sound Source:

A djembe, a conga, a bongo or a trango has mid frequencies and less sustain which means it contains medium or average (neither more nor less) attack time (moderate attack) and less release time(faster release or shorter release).

Note: A chenda or a ghatam contains upper mid frequencies and less than average (moderate) sustain which means it contains less attack time (fast attack) and less release time (faster release or shorter release) but relatively more attack time and release time as compared to the sound sources like shaker or close hi-hat from the drum kit.

Envelope of a Sustained High Frequency Sound Source:

A cymbal, a crash, an open hi-hat from the drum kit, a manjira or a morsing contains high frequencies and more sustain which means it contains less attack time(faster attack or shorter attack) and more release time(slower release or longer release).

Envelope of a transient High Frequency Sound Source:

A shaker or a close hi-hat from the drum kit contains high frequencies and less sustain which means it contains less attack time(faster attack or shorter attack) and less release time(faster release or shorter release).

Note: The velocity and amplitude (loudness) of the sound decreases over time.

1.2.5. Types of a Sound Wave:

a) Longitudinal Waves - The air molecules move along the direction of vibration
b) Transverse Waves - The air molecules move perpendicular to the direction of vibration
c) Propagating Waves - The air molecules move forward to the direction of vibration
d) Standing Waves - The low frequency standing waves stays near by the walls in an indoor area during playback of a low frequency sound

1.2.6. Psychoacoustics:

The study of auditory sensation is known as Acoustics. The perception of sound waves by ear and its psychological effect is known as Psychoacoustics. It investigates the subjective quantities and its relationship with objective quantities.

a) Subjective Quantities - Subjective quantities are the auditory perception by our ears and store informations in our brain for future reference. Pitch, Loudness and Timbre are the examples of subjective quantities.
b) Objective Quantities - An objective quantity can be measured in a meter or an electronic measuring device. The objective quantities are based on logarithmic scale or non-linear scale. Frequency, Sound Pressure Level are the examples of objective quantities.

Sound Measurements of Objective Quantities: Frequency is measured in Hertz. Sound Pressure Level is measured in Decibel.

Relation between objective quantities and subjective quantities:

a) Sound Pressure Level is perceived as Loudness.

b) Fundamental frequency with harmonics and overtones are collectively perceived as Timbre.

c) Change in loudness affects pitch perception by our ears.

d) Frequency is perceived as pitch. Frequencies result Emotions which affect to human health and psychology is described in the following tabulation:

Frequencies in Hertz	Emotion Result
4	Telepathy, Brain's Operating Frequency at sleeping stage
40	Brain's Operating Frequency
285	Rapidly Heals & Regenerate Tissues
396	Remove Guilt, Fear, Balance Root Chakra
417	Body Detox & Cell Purification, Heal & Balance Sacral Chakra, Reverse Negative Effects
432	Ultra Healing Vibration, Raise Positive Vibration, Ease Anxiety, Brings down heart rate and blood pressure
528	DNA Repair & Nerve Regeneration, Heart Chakra Activation, Remove Body Impurities
639	Reconnection & Balancing Relationships, Raise Positive Energy, Attracts Love
741	Cleanse Infections (Virus, Bacteria, Fungal Dissolve Toxins), Electronic Magnetic Radiations, Awaking Intuition
936	Pineal gland Activation
1000	Restore Immune System
2675	Pineal gland Activation

The frequency during normal signal processing by the brain used to be between 12 Hz to 100 Hz also called as beta activity by the brain.

If the human body feels relaxed and surrendered while listening to music then the frequency used to be between 8 Hz to 12 Hz also called as alpha activity by the brain.

If the human body feels relaxed deeply and also feels changeover in body and brain function(such as falling asleep) then the frequency used to be between 4 Hz to 7 Hz also called as theta activity by the brain.

If the human body sleep unconsciously then the frequency used to be between 0.5 Hz to 4 Hz also called as delta activity by the brain.

If the human body feels frustrated, anger, lack of understanding, general dis-satisfication...etc., then the frequency used to be more than 20 KHz.

1.2.7. Noise:

It is an unwanted signal. It exists because of random motion of molecules. It can't be eliminated but can be controlled. It masks the sound which creates distraction.

1.2.7.1. *Types of Noise*:

a) Ambient Noise: It exists naturally and the noise is pleasant.e.g: Waterfall, Seashore… etc.
b) Electrical Noise: It is the noise produced by electronic equipment. It never exist naturally. It is of 2 types -
  (i) Self Noise or Thermal Noise: It occurs because of flow of electrons in the circuits.
  (ii) Handling Noise: It is a Mechanical Vibration because of resonating frequency. It refers to an undesired noise that comes from an electronic audio equipment when being moved or handled (Reason of Handling Noise

could be Electro-static Interference, Electromagnetic Interference, Radio Frequency Interference).

c) Environmental Noise: It is the noise produced while working in the environment. It never exist naturally.

It is of 2 types -

(i) Industrial Noise: A large scale of noise pollution is produced by Industrial Noise such as welding, hammering, drilling, blowing, running machinery, motors, sheet metal work, lathe machine work, operation of cranes, grinding, turning, breaking, steaming, boiling, cooling, heating, painting, pumping, packing, transporting etc.

(ii) Non-Industrial Noise: It is produced during

a) Transportation noise (e.g.:- Aircrafts, Trains, Road Vehicles, Vessels such as Ships and Boats),

b) Residential and Community noise (e.g.:- Electronic Home appliances, Kitchen appliances),

c) Noises at Public Places such as Open Market, Streets, Parks, Railway Stations, Bus stops, Traffic control areas,

d) Noises at Commercial Building (e.g.:- Noises in an Office building such as Lift, Air Conditioners, Keyboard Typing, Xerox-machines, Printers, FAX Machines, Telephone, Document Papers... etc)

1.2.8. Noise Control & its Application:

Noise Control is a set of strategies to reduce noise pollution. It cannot be eliminated but it can be controlled. Therefore, we need proper isolation from noise.

Production cannot be stopped. According to demand of the product, the company has to produce the product in large scale. And the workers need jobs to support their respective family financially.

But the noise degrades health conditions of the workers. So the company provides them ear muffs and ear plugs to protect their ear from the noise while working.

1.2.9. Electronic Components:

1.2.9.1. *Registors*

A good resistor always make sure about the transportation of power or electrical energy with negligible amount of its loss as heat energy. It must be durable and its resistance value mustn't change in the presence of moisture.

Each conductive material has its own resistance. If the resistance is more, less amount of current will flow which interrupt the transportation of power or electrical energy. If the resistance is less, more amount of current will flow which could damage the components of the electronic circuit.

The power through an electronic circuit can be determined by multiplying total voltage across the electronic circuit with the total current flows through that electronic circuit. Ohm's law says, the total voltage across the electronic circuit can be determined by multiplying total resistance or total impedance of the electronic circuit with the total current flows through that electronic circuit. Therefore, we need to pick the right components and design the electronic circuit according to the given power supply.

Unit of resistance is called Ohm. The inverse of resistance is known as Reactance and it's unit is called Mho.

1.2.9.2. *Inductors*

When a current flows through a conductive material, it creates a magnetic field around the direction of flow of current. Similarly, if we place a conductive material at a location having a magnetic field, a certain amount of current (known as induced current) will flow through that conductive material until the magnetic field of that location become inactive.

The inductor in a closed circuit (power supplied to an electronic circuit that contains an inductor) produce its own magnetic field. When the current in an inductor changes, its magnetic field also changes that develop an induced current. That induced current always opposes the change in current of an inductor called self induction.

An inductor doesn't have any effect if a steady current flows in a closed circuit. But the inductor provide an opposing effect if the current value changes. Therefore, an inductor always try to maintain a steady current. During the change in current in a closed circuit, the inductor produces unnecessary heat. So, the inductor coils are made non-inductive. To achieve nearly zero self inductance of the inductor for energy saving, the conductive wire in a closed circuit wound twice on itself that create a structure of an inductor.

An Inductor is good at creating Low Pass Filter which allow you to hear low frequencies by roll-off high frequencies.

An Inductor Based EQ uses Ceramic Core Inductor or Phenolic Core Inductor for high Q-Factor value in High Frequency Applications.

1.2.9.3. *Capacitors*

A certain amount of electrical energy can be stored temporarily in a capacitor (called condenser). In a capacitor, a dielectric medium called insulator, is used to be sandwiched between two oppositely charged conductive materials to avoid any leakage of current. The electrons in an insulator won't leave their parent atoms and molecules even if the insulator placed with in a magnetic field. The conductivity of an insulator placed in a magnetic field is zero or negligible. The insulators (dielectric mediums) such as air, oil, mica, tissue paper... etc are used in capacitors.

Unit of capacitance is called Farad.

A Capacitor is good at creating High Pass Filter which allow you to hear high frequencies by roll-off low frequencies.

1.2.9.4. *Transformers*

An inductor can transfer electrical energy to nearby inductors through electromagnetic principle until we stop providing electrical energy to it.

In a transformer, a power supply used to given to the primary inductor coil that creates magnetic fields. Though a secondary inductor coil is placed with in those magnetic fields, a current is induced or we can say an induced current flows through the secondary inductor coil influenced by those magnetic fields. In a transformer, if the number of turns of primary inductor coil is more than the number of turns of secondary inductor coil, then the transformer is called as a step-down transformer. In a transformer, if the number of turns of secondary inductor coil is more than the number of turns of primary inductor coil, then the transformer is called as a step-up transformer.

Transformer Designs in Microphone Pre-amplifiers:

An audio transformer is used to disconnect external noise and transfer audio signals with out loosing frequencies and their amplitudes. In a microphone preamplifier, we use step-up transformer with a low noise transistor (2G309 by Texas Instruments) that create less or negligible amount of noise which could be in between 1 dB to 1.5 dB. The audio signals inside a microphone pre-amplifier encounters with an operational amplifier at first which feed voltage to the step-up transformer circuit or directed through the cables to the inductor based equaliser and then directed to the step-up transformer. And the audio signal chain is as follows:

> Weak Electrical Mic Signal->Operational Amplifier ->Audio Cable->Inductor based EQ->Stepup Transformer-> Line Level Signal

Transformer Designs in Power supply Amplifiers and Compressors:

The output end of any audio signal processors, power amplifiers, microphone pre-amplifiers should be transformers. A transformer has an amazing advantage of galvanic isolation. We can choose impedances to make a transformer work. The line level signals have both the inductance and capacitance.

A transformer used to have a leakage inductance. If we put a cable line and a transformer together, we get 1dB to 1.5dB of resonance(audible ear pleasant sounds) depends on the length of cable lines. That resonance sounds sweet and musical. If we use an amplifier with out a transformer, the capacitance of the line will cause the amplifier to slew and provide distortion which is a non desirable, non musical sound.

In power supply amplifiers and compressors, we use step-down transformers. that add harmonic contents. In a compressor, a very less amount of audio signal at the input to the transformer adds a little bit of 3rd harmonic contents (odd harmonic contents) at the output of the transformer. More amount of audio signal at the input to that transformer adds more 3rd harmonic contents (odd harmonic contents) and 2nd harmonic contents (even harmonic contents) at the output of the transformer. In a compressor, Nickel based transformer sounds so clean & transparent, Iron based transformer sounds much coloured where as Steel based transformer sounds very dirty.

The modern transformers, reduce feedback of selected frequency band (low or mid) of audible frequencies using feedback winding circuit by manipulating the available feedback parameters of the transformers. To reduce feedback in lower frequency band for a better low frequency response, the Neve Compressor provide Blue Silk circuit. To reduce feedback in mid frequency band for a better mid frequency responses, the Neve Compressor provide Red Silk circuit.

A high amount of current flows all the time through a transformer based Class A amplifier which is useful for tube based circuits, because tube circuits need high supply voltage (300 Volts) for its operation. To extract audio signal from the tube circuit, we need a step-down audio transformer that convert the high supply voltage to a line level signal. In a transformer based class AB amplifier, a high amount of current flows when audio signals are passing through the audio electronic circuit by switching to class A mode; when no audio signals are passing through the audio electronic circuit, the power amplifier switches to class B mode.

Note: In analog telephonic industry, the line level signals used to be applied to telephone lines which further need to be transmitted but 30dB of audio signal loss occurs per 1 mile (1.609344 Kilo-meters). To over come such signal loss several, step-up transformer based power amplifiers were used at each mile of distance between two telephone centres situated at two different places such as villages, towns or cities.

1.2.9.5. *Vacuum Tubes*:

In a vacuum tube, the electrons flow through a highly evacuated glass or metal (1/1000 mm of mercury air pressure) from cathode(that emits electrons) to anode (that collects electrons) in a closed circuit. The flow of electron inside a vacuum tube is unidirectional. The vacuum tube is highly evacuated because

(i) Cathode emits more electrons
(ii) Heated filament won't oxidise and burn
(iii) Presence of air molecules will be ionised and move towards electrode which is undesirable

Vacuum tube (Valve) and Analog Tape Distortion (Saturation) takes away the transient sound (less sustained sound that exist for less time period - a fraction of a second) that our ear never notice but notice the sustained tones because Tube and Analog Tape Distortion introduce even harmonics (e.g.:- 200Hz, 400Hz, 800Hz...etc.).Tube and Analog Tape Distortion sounds rounder and smoother (smoother as per visual perception - a Velvet Cloth material feels smoother if you touch the cloth material or texture of Honey).Products belong to Neve, Harrison companies provide even harmonics distortions. Slower tempo based music such as Blues, Jazz, Classical music... etc contains more sustained instruments that prefer more signal processing of even harmonics distortion.

Note: A diode tube controls polarity of an audio signal. A triode tube is used to amplify weak audio signals. A beam power tube can handle higher sound pressure level at the output stage of an audio amplifier.

Difference between a Triode and a Step-up Transformer:

Both triode and step-up transformer produces voltage amplification. In a step-up transformer, if the voltage is stepped up by a certain ratio, the current is stepped down in the same ratio resulting no power gain. But, if a triode gains the voltage, it gains the current resulting power gain. That is why a loud speaker used to be driven by a triode amplifier instead of a step-up transformer.

Diode Tube as a Rectifier:

A rectifier converts alternating current into direct current. The direct current has one-way path which is suitable for a diode tube. A rectifier is of 2 types.

Half Wave Rectifier: It conducts during one half cycle of alternating current provided at the input of a transformer. At the secondary coil transformer circuit, a single diode tube connected in series with load resistance, are used.

Full Wave Rectifier: It conducts during one full cycle of alternating current provided at the input of a transformer. At the secondary coil centre-tapped transformer circuit, two diode tubes are used.

1.2.9.6. *Discrete Solid State Devices* (Transistors, Operational Amplifiers, Integrated Circuits, Diodes …etc.)

(i) *Semi-conductor Diodes*:

A semi-conductor contains valance bands filled with electrons, conduction bands (that doesn't contain any electron) and a narrow forbidden gap between valance bands and conduction bands. Silicon has a band gap of 1.17 electro-volt. Germanium has a band gap of 0.74 electro-volt. If the narrow forbidden gap between valance bands and conduction bands is absent, then that solid material is called as Insulator. When a potential difference is applied across a semi-conductor or due to thermal collisions at room temperature, some of the electrons flows from valance band to the conduction band.

In a pure-semiconductor (intrinsic), electrons flows from valance band to the conduction band due to thermal collisions at room temperature. In this case, a very small amount of electric current flows. The increase in room temperature pushes more electrons from valance band to the conduction band and results increase in electric conductivity.

In an impure-semiconductor (extrinsic), electrons flows from valance band to the conduction band due to applying potential difference or rise in temperature across the impure-semiconductor. To increase the flow of electric current, a small amount of suitable impurity(called as Dopant) is added. The impurity(Dopant) could be tri-valent (p-type such as Aluminium, Boron, Gallium, Indium) or penta-valent (n-type such as Arsenic, Antimony, Phosphorus).

In an n-type semiconductor, electrons are the majority charge carriers where as in a p-type semiconductor, electrons are the minority charge carriers.

It means we can create resistors, capacitors, transistors and many more electronic components using semiconductor materials and integrate various combinations of these electronic components (operational amplifiers, microphone pre-amplifiers…etc) in a smaller package (portable form), called Integrated Circuit Chips. Please note that a vacuum tube characteristics can also be designed using semiconductor materials. That is why, we are able to use VST, AAX, AU formats based emulated plugins for audio signal processing purposes.

p-n Junction Diode: It conducts electric current in one direction only. A p-n junction can be forward bias when an external voltage is applied in such a way that the potential barrier decreases for easy flow of drift current. Drift current flows due to flow of electrons from valance band to the conduction band after applying potential difference. A p-n junction can be reverse bias when an external voltage is applied in such a way that the potential barrier increases for a very less flow of reverse current.

p-n Junction Diode as a Rectifier:

A rectifier converts alternating current into direct current. The direct current has one-way path which is suitable for a p-n junction diode. A rectifier is of 2 types.

Half Wave Rectifier: It conducts during one half cycle of alternating current provided at the input of a transformer. At the secondary coil transformer circuit, a single p-n junction diode connected in series with load resistance are used.

Full Wave Rectifier: It conducts during one full cycle of alternating current provided at the input of a transformer. At the secondary coil centre-tapped transformer circuit, two p-n junction diode are used.

Zener Diode: It is a p-n junction diode designed specially to operate in Zener Breakdown region of reverse voltage characteristics. It is made up of heavily doped acceptor and donor impurities in p-n junction diode. In this case, Silicon is preferred over Germanium because of its higher temperature and current capability. Because of heavily doped acceptor and donor impurities, the depletion layer between p-type and n-type materials becomes very thin and reverse bias voltage increases beyond certain limit (Zener Breakdown Voltage) resulting increase in reverse current sharply.

A Zener diode is used as a voltage regulator, peak clipper, fixed reference voltage in a network for biasing and comparison purposes, used for calibrating volt meters. We also do find Zener diodes in Limiter(a dynamic processor).

A semi-conductor diode is a non-linear device with a huge amount of distortion and generate a huge amount of heat. But if we configure it in a bridge format, we can get rid of those distortion. Once the diode is configured in a bridge format, then we can apply audio signals across one set of contacts and we can apply a control voltage across the other side of contacts. By choosing the limit of control and signal, it give quite a good account of itself. Thus the diode bridge configuration can be used as a control element of the compressor. If we use the same configuration in reverse to derive a control voltage, we can use the amplifier available to us. The output stage that we used to drive the lines in the analog console could be the transformer based line amplifier with some minor changes in the configuration to change the sound pressure level of each channel strip of the analog console.

Rupert Neve had made a diode bridge compressor (2252, 2253 and 2254) in a modular format for abc television's analog console purchased in 1969 and replaced the limiter-compressor manufactured by Pie (one of the Phillips company) which lacked reliability. The diode bridge compressor has a great amount of control by providing a nice control curve and a very sweet sounding compressor. The built-in limiter of the diode bridge compressor is virtually a brick wall limiter.

(ii) *Transistors*:

Both conductor based and semi-conductor based transistors always introduce odd harmonics (e.g.:- 100Hz, 300Hz, 500Hz... etc.).Transistor sounds buzzier (grainy as per visual perception - a premium Raymond Cloth Material feels grainy if you touch the cloth material or texture of Sugar).Mid frequencies and high frequencies (treble sound) can be easily manipulated to make it sound grainy, upfront, prominent, audible, identifiable by using transistor based audio equipments. Products belong to SSL, API companies provides odd harmonics distortions. Medium tempo and faster tempo based music such as Pop, Rock music...etc contains less sustained instruments (transient sounds) that prefer more signal processing of odd harmonics distortion.

Note:- Sine Waves don't contain any harmonics. Triangular Waves contain Even Harmonics(2nd-order Harmonics) and Square Waves contain Odd Harmonics (3rd-order Harmonics).

A transistor is a solid-state version of triode vacuum tube. It transfers a signal from low resistance region to high resistance region. It is of two types - unipolar transistor (Field Effect Transistor) and bipolar transistor (Junction Transistors).

The conductivity of a unipolar transistor (Field Effect Transistor) is due to only one type of majority charge carriers (flow of electrons or holes). The electric field causes the electrons to move in the unipolar transistor.

The conductivity of a bipolar transistor (Junction Transistor) is due to both majority charge carriers and minority charge carriers (flow of electrons and holes). A bipolar transistor has two p-n junctions. A bipolar transistor is two types: p-n-p transistor and n-p-n transistor. Such bipolar transistors has three layers - emitter, base and collector. The base is used to sandwiched between emitter and collector.

Note: Maintaining a suitable voltage across two junctions of a transistor is called biasing. During the operation of a transistor, the emitter-base junction is always forward bias and the collector-base junction is reverse biased.

Among the modes of transistors, the common base and common emitter transistors can be used as amplifiers. But modern transistors are very small and can't dissipate more heat like vacuum tube does. So the transistor based audio electronic circuit or integrated circuits goes through the techniques that generates distortion. An integrated circuit contains a complementary power supply amplifier with two devices (class A and class B) at its output that shares the load by switching one to the other which generates a crossover distortion containing frequencies that at not a part of any harmonics and also not related to audible frequencies. Transistors has a bad reputation for reliability because we always use our audio equipments for a longer period of time and the transistors can't handle large amount of current. During thermal runaway, the transistor gets hotter by drawing more current and at the end the transistor blows. Therefore, we replaced transistors with semi-conductors. But manufacturing semi-conductors is much expensive.

At an ideal case, one device handling audio signals in the positive quadrant and the other device handling audio signals in the negative quadrant. The transistor based audio electronic circuit or integrated circuit can't handle high power and higher voltage (300 Volts) supplied to it. To maintain low power and low voltage (24 Volts) in the integrated circuit, we need to make it run a lower amount of current. As a result, the power supply amplifier switches from class A mode to class B mode. The two curves don't cross over at the middle that generate a crossover distortion containing frequencies that at not a part of any harmonics and also not related to audible frequency band.

(iii) *Integrated Circuits*:

An integrated circuit contains many semiconductor based electronic components (resistors, capacitors, transistors...etc) packaged in a small enclosure. It uses less energy because of using a reduced transportation of electric current (that consumes more heat energy, a converted form of electric energy). It produces crossover distortion. The new design for 5088 analog console by Neve is to avoid crossover distortion and slew rate distortion by custom designed dedicated discrete operational amplifier or integrated circuit with class-A single sided for audio signal processing. For a greater dynamic range, the integrated circuit needed a higher supply voltage (90 Volts) that creates 10 to 12 dB of additional headroom. So, the goals of designing should be having low distortion & low noise with a few semi-conductors and must be reliable.

According to the theory of Audio Electronics, quality of audio components use in each audio equipment, circuit design for the purpose of audio production applications are important factors and the reviews of audio tools and audio equipments are as follows:

1.2.9.7. *Audio Cables and Connectors:*

The audio signals can be transferred through the conductors of audio cables because the outer electrons of each atom and molecule moves freely throughout the outer surface of conducting material but won't leave the conducting material. The impedance of good quality of audio cables and audio components used to be 600 Ohms to maintain frequency response from 30 Hertz (30 cycles per second) to 15 KHz (15000 cycles per second) throughout the audio signal chain (from input to the output).

Each connector of an audio cable results 5% loss of original signal. Therefore, an audio cable contains two audio connectors, resulting 10% loss of original signal. To compensate the loss of audio signals, we use amplifiers at the input and output audio signal chains.

But an optical cable transmits 100% of signals because of Total Internal Reflections (e.g:- A cloud in the sky looks white and bright in colour because of bending of sun light by water drops of cloud). The signal loss happens based on distance in kilometres between light transmitter and receiver and the connectors used in the fibers.

Good quality audio cables and connectors are provided by the companies like Neutrik, Moogami, Klotz, World Wind, Belden, SOMMER. Medium quality audio cables and connectors are provided by the companies such as Krystal and MX.

1.2.9.8. *Output Transducers:*

If you are purchasing a pair of Reference Studio Monitors (Speakers) or Headphones, the features must be present as follows:

1. The speaker amplifiers must have a good Damping Factor (e.g:- Speaker Manufacturer such as Focal, Barefoot Sound, PMC, Quested, Dynaudio, Genelec, Tannoy, Meyer Sound, Martin Audio provides great damping factor).A damping factor is the ability of an amplifier to control unwanted motion of the speaker. A high damping factor of a loud speaker management system tells us that the speaker amplifier's impedance absorbs the electricity generated by the speaker coil motion and stops unnecessary speaker's vibration (reducing the sound pressure levels or loudness produced by the movements of speaker drivers' diaphragm because of its own inertia after the signal stops).

2. The speaker's input impedance must match with the output impedance of your mixer, audio interface or playback system that you use. Impedance Matching is necessary to drive the sound properly and make the sound audible correctly.

3. A speaker's output frequency range must be more than that of our audible frequency range (20Hz to 20KHz) so that it can provide a precise sound to judge during audio signal processing.

4. Always try to find a pair of right speakers suitable for your room. The size of each speaker driver for a Home Studio must be 6 inches to 9 inches. If you are not able to find the right speakers for your room or if your room size, room shape, room dimension are not correct to listen from entry level of a pair of professional speakers or if you travel a lot, then use a headphone.

5. When you play a sound in your left speaker, you can locate the sound at left side because the left speaker is closer to your left ear as compared to right ear. But you can hear the sound by both of your ears while playing a sound to your left speaker. The softer sound that you hear to your right ear while playing a sound to your left speaker is called as "Crosstalk" which is not available for a headphone by default. As per the technology developed, crosstalk feature is also available to the

headphone. Using impulse response audio sample recorded at any studio containing the room information and using binaural processing for crosstalk feature, we have a privilege to experience any popular studio environment, speakers and microphones used in those studios using a headphone and technology resulting a digital product as a software plugin that incorporate binaural processing and impulse response of popular studio environments.

Speakers:

Manufacturers such as ADAM, Focal are useful for Audio Playback. Focal speakers used to have a very high damping factor. Most of the ADAM speakers use ribbon tweeters that make us listen for longer period of time.

Manufacturers such as PMC, Kali Audio are useful for Audio Tracking during Sound Recording. Such products used to have an average damping factor which provide a huge and open sound.

Manufacturers such as Tannoy, Genelec, Neumann, Barefoot, Quested, ATC, Altec are useful for Audio Post-production (Sound Editing, Sound Mixing and Sound Mastering).

Manufacturers of cheapest loud speaker amplifiers and loud speakers including bass frequency drivers used to have a very low damping factor which need an outboard compressor unit to increase the damping factor for calibration purpose.

Headphones:

Beyerdynamics DT 990 Pro:

1. Popular among Musicians, Music Producers and Beginners for listening playback of their respective favourite Pop and Rock music
2. Bass and Treble are mildly boosted with taking care of proper balance between them.

3. This headphone is useful for listening the playback of medium tempo songs and music such as Pop and Rock Music

Audio Technica ATH M70x:

1. Popular among Signal Tracking and Tracing Engineers, Live Mix Engineers (Front of House System Engineers)
2. Useful for Forensic applications
3. Purpose: Audio Signal Processing in a noisy environment at both indoor and outdoor concert venues

AKG K712 Pro:

1. Popular among Sound Editors, Mixing Engineers, Mastering Engineers during Audio Post-production because All India Radio Stations and National Television Stations used to bulk import AKG products.
2. It gives maximum wearing comfort for fatigue free mixing and mastering with improved low end performance.
3. Purpose: Audio Signal Processing in a noise-controlled environment such as Edit Suites, Recording Studios, Mixing Studios, Mastering Suites
4. Purpose: Useful for those who love to experience 'Premium Graded Sound' during playback listen

Beyerdynamics DT 880 Pro:

1. Popular among Sound Editors, Mixing Engineers, Mastering Engineers during audio post-production
2. Purpose: Audio Signal Processing in a noise-controlled environment such as Edit Suites, Recording Studios, Mixing Studios, Mastering Suites
3. This headphone is useful for listening the playback of slow tempo songs and music such as Jazz Music and Classical Music

Note: The diaphragm of each transducer experiences damping forces due to friction and resistance of air medium

1.2.9.9. *Input Transducers*

Please refer page number 81 to 88.

1.2.9.10. *Computer Machines:*

In a computer machine, you need to take care of the following requirements:

If you like to make electronic music or design the electronic sound using emulated digital synthesisers plugins, then your CPU must have more catche memory. It means, your microprocessors manufactured by Intel, Apple, Qualcomm or AMD processors must have more catche memory.

If you like to make music using sampled musical instruments' library or want to use for the purpose of video rendering, then you must upgrade your RAM and storage spaces of your computer machine.

If you are a student of an audio engineering institute or just started learning or providing services for sound recording, sound editing, mixing, mastering, then your existing computer machine has enough power, specifications and support system to complete your audio production tasks. But you must learn about troubleshooting to solve common and general problems. Operating systems such as Ubuntu Studio and macOS are preferred for more stability and hardware compatibility than Windows operating system.

1.2.9.11. *Analog and Digital Audio Workstations:*

Introduction to Analog Work Stations and Digital Work Stations: An Analog Work Station contains

1. a rack mount of analog tape recorders for feeding the recorded analog signal to the Mix Desk,

2. a Mix Desk (Mixing Console) for feeding the recorded analog signal to the Audio Signal Processors according to the skilful mix engineers,
3. a rack mount of Audio Signal Processors,
4. other accessories such as a scissor tool and a pencil tool (marker tool) for editing the analog tapes.

A Digital Audio Work Station contains

1. Edit Window (Arrange Window, Sequence Window) - In this workspace, we can find audio regions (audio clips) on audio tracks and MIDI regions (MIDI clips) on MIDI tracks. We do tracking the input signals from the microphones, line instruments and triggering equipments(MIDI Devices or Controllers) in this edit window.
2. Inspector Section - In this workspace, we can monitor the audio signals and audio signal processing of selected audio track or MIDI track.
3. Mix Window - It behaves just like a Traffic Control System. We do tracing, routing, signal processing of all audio channels in this mix window. In this workspace, we mix the audio signals just the way we cook dishes for different flavours by putting a certain amount of hot taste such as a certain amount of chilli and pepper (a certain amount of loudness of Bass Instruments such as Kick and Bass), a certain amount of sour taste such as a certain amount of tamarind and lemon (a certain amount of loudness of Lower-mid Frequency produced Instruments such as Toms and Hand Percussions such as Djambe, Pakhawaj... etc), a certain amount of salty taste such as a certain amount of salt (a certain amount of loudness of Upper-mid Frequency produced Instruments such as Vocals, Violins, Chenda), a certain amount of sweet taste such as a certain amount of sweet dessert, chocolate and ice-cream (a certain amount of loudness of Treble Instruments such as shaker, cymbals and crashes)

4. Transport Bar - In this workspace, we can find different buttons to play, pause, record, stop, forward, rewind, cycle play the audio production session and also we find different display sections to setup Tempo, Sample Rate, Bit Depth, Time Code, Time Signature, Key Scale informations.

5. Tool Bar - It is a tools' pallet in the audio editor which contains Marque Tool, Scissor Tool, Fade Tool, Hand Tool, Trim Tool, Gain Tool, Automation Tool, Pencil Tool.

6. Media Browser - To browse and import any media files (Audio files, MIDI files, Video files)

7. Loop Browser - To browse the audio loops of any instrument that plays according to the key scale and tempo that we set for our audio project.

8. Audio Editor - In this workspace, we can time correct, pitch correct the audio if pitch and tempo related problems exists. We can also do basic edits like cut, copy, paste, fade, trim...etc.

9. Piano Roll (MIDI Editor) - In this workspace, we can time correct, pitch correct the MIDI events if pitch and tempo related problems exists. We can also do basic edits like cut, copy, paste, fade, trim, melody tune creation...etc.

1.2.9.12. *Analog Magnetic Tape Recorder Machine:*

The signature tape recorder sound can be achieved as follows:

1. *Magnetic Tape Formula Type of Magnetic Tape*:

   a) 250 provides an oldest sound signature, can be easily saturated, controls high frequencies in a better way, roll of transients, useful for sounds like snare

   b) 900 provide a modern sound signature, can handle lower frequencies in a better way

2.   *Magnetic Tape Speed*: It acts like an Equaliser.

Slower Tape Speed (e.g:- 7.5 IPS) felt increase in low frequencies than high frequencies. In case of 7.5 inches per second, the highest frequencies peaks at 17 KHz. It can be applicable for High frequency sounds.

Faster Tape Speed (e.g:- 15 IPS) felt increase in high frequencies than low frequencies. In case of 15 inches per second, the highest frequencies peaks at an octave higher than 17 KHz. It can be applicable for Low frequency sounds.

3. *Calibration:* It acts like a Distortion unit.

Its lower value indicates less Harmonics addition which is useful for transient sounds (e.g:- Snare Drum)

Its higher value indicates more Harmonics addition which is useful for sustained sounds (e.g:- Violin)

4.   Secondary Controls: We can control the internal electronic circuit parameters for calibration and post tape play-head processing purposes.

a) *Repro EQ*: While recording on a Magnetic Tape Machine, the record head cut off high frequencies at the rate of 6 dB per octave where as the play head recover the loss of high frequencies using Repro Equaliser during playback. The HF and LF parameters of Repro EQ control the tone (frequency response) at the tape machine's playhead output and its playback curve is as follows:

(i)   NAB (American), It increases High Frequencies above 3 KHz and boosts also Low Frequencies. It can be applicable for Low frequency sounds.

(ii) CCIR (European), It increases only High Frequencies above 6.3 KHz. It can be applicable for High frequency sounds.

b) *Sync EQ*: The HF and LF parameters of Repro EQ control the tone (frequency response) at the tape machine's record head input

c) *BIAS*: It acts like a Transformer based Low Level Compressor that provide strength to the weaker audio signals.

More BIAS provide more strength to the weaker audio signals. Too much increase of bias results Saturation (Harmonic Distortion) and cutoff peak loudness of transient sounds which is useful for softer sustained sounds

Less BIAS provide less strength to the weaker audio signals, useful for louder transient sounds to control peak loudness of transient sounds

d) *HF Driver*: To drive more high frequencies.

e) *GANG CTRLS*: To group all tape machine's parameters

f) *Machine Modes*:
   (i) *Thru Mode*: Bipass Button
   (ii) *Input Mode:* Monitoring Mode
   (iii) *Sync Mode*: Listening through Record Head
   (iv) *Repro Mode*: Listening through tape recorder with post Tape Playhead Processing

For a Kick Drum, we apply less Bias with NAB Repro EQ at the rate of higher Magnetic Tape Speed (15 IPS)

For a Bass Guitar, we apply more Bias with NAB Repro EQ at the rate of higher Magnetic Tape Speed (15 IPS)

for a Closed Hi-hat, we apply less Bias with CCIR Repro EQ at the rate of slower Magnetic Tape Speed (7.5 IPS)

For a Violin, we apply more Bias with CCIR Repro EQ at the rate of slower Magnetic Tape Speed (7.5 IPS)

DAW Products:

Protools by Avid

1. Popular among Sound Recordists and Sound Editors

2. Special Features: The way C++ programming language used for creating Protools Work Station, is incredible in storing digital format of recorded audio datas

Logic Pro by Apple

1. Popular among Music Producers and Music Composers
2. Special Features: Its workspaces are properly organised, all type of audio signal processors are available, sound designing and audio signal processing are simple to use

Ableton

1. Popular among Disk Jockeys, Music Performers during live sound reinforcement (in live concert environments)
2. Special Features: Great transient response of the percussions and drum kits during audio playback, quick loops and sample loading of the instruments as compared to other Digital Audio Workstations

Reason Studios by Propellerhead

1. Popular among Songwriters, Music Composers, Music Programmers (who use MIDI instruments), Musicians, Singers
2. Designed for skilful Sound Recordists and Audio Post-production Engineers (Sound Editors, Mix Engineers, Mastering Engineers) for medium tempo songs such as Pop music and Rock music
3. Special Features: Allow the user to focus more on Music Making by taking care of sound designing and audio signal processing as compared to Logic Pro

Cubase & Nuendo by Steinberg

1. Cubase is popular among Sound Editors and music programmers where as Nuendo is Popular among Audio Post-production Engineers
2. Special Features: Music Scoring, Sound Editing of audio for audio-visuals (Films, TV Series, Web Series, Documentaries, Ad Films, Corporate Videos, Video Tutorials... etc)

Mixbus by Harrison

1. Popular among skilful Mix Engineers and Mastering Engineers
2. Special Features: Less chance of system (CPU) overload. It can run in any configuration of computer hardware system in any Operating System.
3. Special Features: It gives an analog sound ('even harmonics' for 'silky smooth' sounding) on digital domain, mixing can be done very quickly because of a well planned smart workspace created with knob per function layout.

Reaper by Cockos

1. Popular among skilful Audio Post-production Engineers (Sound Editors, Mix Engineers, Mastering Engineers)
2. Special Features: Less chance of system (CPU) overload. It can run in any configuration of computer system in any Operating System.
3. Special Features: It allows the user to do any kind of combinations of signal processing using available tools which means it gives freedom to make and break the rules to achieve your goals

FL Studio by Image-Line

1. Popular among the Rappers, Singers, Music Programmers, Hip-hop Music Producers
2. Caution: The user need to rely on third-party tools for audio signal processing

1.2.10. Audio Sampler & Sequencer:

Usually, your music idea will stay in your brain for a few minutes and it vanishes, which is difficult to remember. For that, you need to get your music out of your head and manifest into a tangible form very quickly, if the samples are recorded the way it should be to produce a natural and cohesive sound (including the room sound, which is an important part of the sound produced by a sound source) using the recording process and the musical instrument sample production companies are working in that direction beautifully by collaborating with Professional Musicians under the guidance of skilful Music Conductors, Music Supervisors, Music Composers, Record Producers, Sound Recordists, Mix Engineers and Mastering Engineers.

One of the goals of musical instrument sample production companies is to make the musical samples of any programmable sound source, able to get your musical ideas (your vision) realised, manifested or materialised as soon as possible. Thus, your musical ideas played and programmed with different instruments and converted in an audible musical piece very quickly with a natural and cohesive room sound. The instrument plugins are designed based on a dedicated fully lossless audio compression system to save more drive space.

The musical instrument sample production companies such as Spitfire Audio, Orchestral Tools, Soniccouture, Project SAM, pianobook, Native Instruments ...etc provides free, high quality oriented instrument samples with MIDI Sampler or MIDI Sequencer, which were recorded in a dedicated studio space that sounds cohesive (you don't need to even think about mixing process of your programmed MIDI tracks, which has saved much time on figuring out audio signal processing for mixing).

Kontakt by Native Instruments:

1. Special Features: It trigger the samples and playback of those samples are precise.
2. Special Features: Sample libraries of instruments made for this sampler are quality oriented. The name of a few third party sample libraries for Kontakt are as follows:

Cine Orch by Cine Samples, Cine Brass Pro by Cine Samples, Cine Wind Pro by Cine Samples, Voxos by Cine Samples, Cine Brass Pro by Cine Samples, Tina Guo by Cine Samples, Drum of War2 by Cine Samples, Box of Trix by Soniccouture, Ondes by Soniccouture, Martenot by Soniccouture, Xtended Piano by Soniccouture, Array Mbiramby Soniccouture, Nova Chord by Soniccouture, Cinematic Guitars by Sample Logic, Cinematic Keys by Sample Logic, Cimbalom by Spitfire, BML Horn Section by Spitfire, Abby Road 50s Drummer, Abby Road 80s Drummer, Abby Road 70s Drummer, Abby Road 60s Drummer, Chris Hein Winds Volume 1, Chris Hein Winds Volume 2, Chris Hein Winds Volume 3, Chris Hein Winds Volume 4, Chris Hein Horns Volume 1.5, Chris Hein Horns Volume 2, Chris Hein Horns Volume 3, Chris Hein Horns Volume 4, Altus, Shevannai, Voice of Gaia Strawberry, Soundinn Venus, Cinematic Guitars, Cage Brass, Nitron, Requiem, Emotional Piano, Chris Hein Horns(All Volumes), Chris Hein Horn Vol. 2, Orchestral Brass Classic, Symphobia, The Elements, Exhale, Adagio by Violas, Mystica, Female Chamber, Cuba, Epic Cinematic Drums and Sound Design, Scarbee Rickenbocker, Bass, Studio Drummer, Discovery Series West Africa, Scarbee Vintage Keys, Evolve Mutation 2, Alicia's Keys, vir2 Acou6stics, Symphobia Colours Animator, Symphobia Colours Orchestrator, Cantus Georgian Chants, Action Strikes, LUMINA by Project SAM, Geosonics, Morpheus, Accordions,

Orchestral Brass Classic by Project SAM, Spitfire Percussion, Epic Frame Drum Ensemble, Plucked Grand Piano, Sonokinetic tutti, Sable Strings, Sable Strings Vol.2, Cage Brass, Toccata, Latin World, Boesendorfer290, Colossus ...and many more.

The product, BBC Orchestra by Spitfire Audio, has built-in sampler, sample libraries and different miking position features. They have recorded each instrument through different miking positions at AIR Studios in London and sounds awesome, when you load BBC Orchestra in an instrument track, select one of the instruments and start playing on your MIDI instrument(MIDI Sitar, MIDI Guitar, MIDI Keyboard).

Decent Sampler by Decidedly:

Is is an alternative sampler of Kontakt Sampler that supports, iPadOS, macOS, Windows, Linux, Android OS and most of the DAWs with VST, AU, AAX formats

1.2.11. Audio Interfaces:

It converts the analog signals from the input, into digital signals at a resolution (time domain in analog form converted into sample rate digitally and amplitude or loudness of the analog waveform converted into bit-depth digitally), fixed by the user, which can be stored into a computer through a file management folder system. It also converts the digital signals, stored at a file management folder system of a computer, into analog signals to provide an analog output for playback purpose at the same resolution. It can also do both analog to digital and digital to analog conversions at the same time period.

Most of the audio interfaces and playback systems, that has digital to analog converters, try to reduce jitter noise by introducing a buffer which works for some how but the jitter noise appears again because of bad clock, bad power supply, power connected to a different outlet, use of too long and too short cables, bad receiver... etc. Jitter noise matters more for musicians (specially the drummers and percussionists) and a regular listener of music, who sense perfect pitch.

The digital to analog converter of an audio interface or a playback systems must have low phase errors or low phase noise (we need an electronic chip having low phase errors) with an excellent quality of a clock generator (a nice clean crystal oscillator that generate a clock signal).We want both the clock signal and the converted digital samples to analog signal, must be in sync and extremely accurate for a short time period. Due to change in voltage, if the digital samples are a little early or little late, a distortion or jitter appears. The manufacturing company of an audio interface shouldn't bother about synchronisation accuracy of sampled datas with the clock signal for a longer time period because accuracy for a longer time period matters for a Global Positioning System so that it won't get any wrong information.

Saffire series by Focusrite:

1. Popular among the Songwriters, Singers, Musicians, Music Composers, Music Arrangers, Sound Recordists, Music Producers
2. Purpose: Audio Signal Processing from the Artists to their Listeners to maintain transparency technically between the artists (performers) and the listeners
3. Special Features: Sound Recording and Monitoring

Apollo Series & VOLT Series by Universal Audio:

1. Popular among the skilful Sound Recordists, Sound Editors, Mix Engineers (for both Live and Studio Environments), Mastering Engineers, Professional Musicians who has at least 10 years of good experiences in their respective professions
2. Purpose: Audio Signal Processing from the artist to the listeners to maintain transparency technically between the artists (performers) and the listeners

3. Special Features: Any frequency ranges can be manipulated from the audible frequency ranges using a perfect marriage of hardware (audio interface) and software (analog emulated plugins)

DigiGrid D:

1. Popular among the Live Mix Engineers (Front of House Engineers), Signal Tracking and Tracing Engineers
2. Purpose: Audio Signal Processing from the artist to the listeners to maintain transparency technically between the artists (performers) and the listeners
3. Special Features: Any frequency ranges can be manipulated from the audible frequency ranges using analog emulated plugins independently.

Audient iD4, iD14 & iD22:

1. Popular among the Songwriters, Singers, Guitar Players, Musicians
2. Purpose: Sound Recording and Sound Editing by the Artist

Native Instruments Komplete Audio 6 & Arturia Minifuse Series:

1. Popular among the Live MIDI (Musical Instrument Digital Interface) Instrument Players, Music Composers, Songwriters
2. Special Feature: Availability of good instrument libraries by Native Instruments

Impact Twin by tc electronic, Motu Ultralite MK3 & MK4:

1. Popular among the Live Sound Engineers, Musicians, Monitor Mix Engineers, Signal Tracking and Tracing Engineers
2. Purpose: Audio Signal Processing during Jamming Sessions of Musicians (Artists, Performers), Monitor Mix Engineers

Tascam US 2x2, Behringer Uphoria Series:

1. Popular among the Sound Engineers and Sound Editors
2. Purpose: Sound Recording and Sound Editing

M-Audio M Track 2x2 M, M Track Eight, M Track Plus II:

1. Popular among the Songwriters, Singers, Musicians and Sound Recordists
2. Purpose: Sound Recording and Sound Editing by the Artists and Sound Recordists

1.2.11.1. *Digital Audio Signal Converter Chips:*

AKM add colors and sounds very dynamic and rounded. It's range of frequency manipulation's and enhancements are huge including the bass frequencies. It is used by Audient and MOTU Audio Interface Manufacturers

Cirrus Logic sounds a bit nebulous, cloud-like presentation but pleasant. It is used by UAD VOLT SERIES, Antelope ZEN GO Synergy Core, BEHRINGER, ARTURIA, TASCAM, FOCUSRITE, Black Lion Audio Revolution Audio Interface Manufacturers

Wolfson (owned by Cirrus Logic) gives a nice bite. It is used by Apple iPod Classic

ESS add colors which is useful for vocals and casual listening. It also sounds edgy and a bit upfront but little harsh at higher frequencies. It is used by RME Babyface Pro FS Audio Interface.

Sabre *also* sounds edgy

Burr Brown sounds smooth with more detailing

Philips Bitstream gives a non stop assault of mediocre sound

Note: The statements on Digital Audio Signal Converter Chips are based on listening experiences of Audio Professionals. A lot of what we hear has more to do with the end stage output (such as the opamps and related circuitry) than the digital front end too. So there is no direct comparison to say that an AKM chip sounds 'mellower' than a ESS chip unless the circuitry and end stage amplification designs and components are identical. Few Computer Gaming Motherboard Manufacturers like Gigabyte allows operational amplifier integrated chip (opamp IC chip) swapping or replacing at audio driver unit at the motherboards.

CHAPTER 1.3

OBSERVATIONAL SKILLS' DEVELOPMENT

1.3.1. Introduction

A consumer always care about the visuals, speeches, dialogues and lyrics from the digital media contents because they trigger the magical moments of his/her life.

A consumer never care about the environment where he/she is listening. Most of the listeners love to use a mobile phone and an ear phone to access the digital media contents because of portability and availability of those contents instantly through mobile applications and streaming services.

The audio visual contents has been provided in the following different platforms to the consumers:

1. Internet
2. Radio and Television Broadcasting
3. Audio Visual Store Vendors
4. Live Performances at Drama Theatre Shows & Musical Shows

The audio visual contents has been provided in the following different environment to the consumers:

1. Portable Devices such as mobile phones, laptops, tablets… etc.
2. Radios and Televisions
3. Physical Products such as LP Records, Cassettes, CDs, DVDs, Greeting Cards, Musical Toys… etc.
4. Movie Theatres
5. Live Shows such as Drama Theatre Shows, Live Musical Shows

The quality of contents can be experienced very well at Live Show Venues and Movie Theatres than the available portable digital devices. If you watch a movie on your mobile phone, that you have seen recently at a movie theatre or if you watch a musical show broadcasted on your television, that you have experienced recently at the live show venue, then you might find a huge difference on your experiences because of change in environments. A movie theatre or a live show venue looks quite bigger than a palace or castle. In a movie theatre, people watch the movies on a bigger screen and they are surrounded by many speakers. In a live show venue, people watch the performances of the actors, dancers, tour musicians, singers and they are also surrounded by many line-array speakers and cluster of speakers. You can create such an environment at home to experience the quality of audio visual contents by investing your valuable time, money and knowledge.

1.3.2. Learn to Listen:

We have different kind of listening experiences. As a member of general public, we listen to music for pleasure that triggers our emotions such as happiness, sadness, anger, passion, gratefulness... etc. But as a member of music production team, we listen to music technically and spy others' hit records for analysis of current trends and create databases which help to plan and work for the future projects. It will be helpful, if we listen the musical contents parallely in both emotionally way and technical way.

Kinesthetics Observation is the observation we study about the movement of human body such as laughing, crying, increase & decrease of heart rate or breathing, raising eyebrows, gasping, foot tapping, finger snapping, hands clapping, dancing, head bobbing, tilting head to one side, putting hands on your face, goose bumps, getting chills, biting lips... etc. Through such human body responses, you can clearly judge your music.

When you perform live in front of your audience as an artist or a live mix engineer, you need to observe whether your listeners respond positively or not. If your audience is not laughing, crying, gasping, foot tapping, finger snapping, hands clapping, dancing, head bobbing.. etc, then you need to communicate with your band mates and the mix engineer to make it happen by executing your backup plan instantly such as 'switching to a different time signature, different key scale, different groove or rhythm pattern after the bridge or the instrumental solo' or 'performing next an upbeat tempo song' or 'shuffling the order of your songs in your playlist' or review the technical requirements on the sound mixing console such as compressing the drum sound a bit, increasing reverb on snare and guitars that plays open chords so that your listeners will respond positively; as a result your listeners are engaged with the artist's performance or activity.

As a sound recordist in studio environment, you need to observe your artist's body response to trace the errors such as loudness of the sound in the artist's headphone at vocal booth is much more or very less, height of the microphone stand or notation stand is very less or too much, your artist might need a break to drink water because of change in vocal texture.

As a mix engineer, you need to observe the kinesthetics response of your record producers, mastering engineers, clients by playback the music and need to note down which part of the musical piece doesn't work and ask for a verbal feedback for it so that you can rework on it. In this way, you can learn and grow quickly.

As a monitor mix engineer in a live performance venue nearby the stage, you need to observe your each artist's body response to trace the errors such as loudness of other artists' instruments' sound in each artist's headphone or nearby monitors on the stage is much more or very less, phase cancellation of a particular instrument's sound by the monitors at the artist's sitting or standing location on the stage.

1.3.3. Listening Skill Development:

A song or a musical-piece contains genre, tempo, dynamics, rhythm, time signature, key scale and a number of musical instruments' performances including vocal performances.

A musical genre of a song can be identified according to the tempo and the musical instruments used in it. At slower tempo, most of the musical instruments used in the song produce more sustained sound and more towards bass sound in general. At faster tempo, most of the musical instruments used in the song produce less sustained sound (transient sound) and more towards treble sound in general. Timbre allows us to identify two different instruments playing the same note.

A tempo indicates number of beats per minute.e.g:- 120 BPM means 120 beats per minute (60 seconds)i.e. 2 beats per second. A constant tempo feels boring or dullness to the listener where as a variable tempo create interest to listen the song for experiencing a constant pleasure, because the tempo is also a form of expression. When you hear a song by a music band live at the concert venue, it feels far better than the same song in a music video released by them because the tempo is not constant every time during performing live. In old western classical songs, you might have observed the slowing down of tempo at a pause and speeding up of tempo after that pause because the music conductor has instructed so or the drummer/percussionist has played so. In Carnatic Music and Dance Performances, you might have observed the slowing down of tempo at a pause and speeding up of tempo after that pause because the mridangam player has played so. You might also have observed slowing down of tempo a bit, when the mridangam player has played the rhythm louder or softer at twice speed (2X speed) to grab the attention of listeners or viewers towards the aggressive or pleasant expression of dancers or the aggressive or pleasant expression of lyrics.

A live performance is always dynamic in nature which create interest in the listeners or viewers. Dynamics is a form of expression and help to tell a story. For a pleasant expression of a dancer or a lyrics (such as love, sorrow), the sound of the music used to be very soft, but for an aggressive or serious expression of the dancer or a lyrics (such as anger, worries), the sound of the music used to be very loud and played at a bit of faster tempo. Sometimes, dynamics is used to create tension and release. A typical example of dynamics is that you start your intro soft, slowly build dynamics through the verse, thus creating some tension, and release the loudest part of your song at the chorus. The larger the dynamic jumps between sections, the more of a dynamic range you will have.

A Rhythm is the arrangement of sounds as they move through time. Each sound (note and chord) has a given time where the sound is on or off. In the music, this time value is known as note length or rhythm notation. And note lengths are related to time signature.

A time signature indicates number of divisions per 1 bar and number of repetition in one cycle. e.g:- In 6/4 time signature, there are 6 divisions in 1 bar and number of playing of musical piece in one complete cycle is one. The number 4 indicates the number of quarters in one cycle. In 6/8 time signature, the number of quarters in one cycle is 8, so the number of playing of musical piece in one complete cycle is twice. Therefore, at twice speed of the tempo the musical piece will be repeated twice to complete one bar. In 6/16 time signature, the musical piece will be repeated four times at four time speed of the tempo to complete one bar.

Generally, a song is based on one key scale. Sometimes a song is based on two key scales. The second key scale you can find at first verse onwards after intro, at second verse or at outro-chorus. Key-scale need to be determined according to the singable range of the vocalist or playable range of a lead musical instrument. Key scale for a background score used to be decided by the Music Conductor where as the key scale for a song used to be decided by the Music Arranger, Music Director or a Record Producer.

Note: The ears of people, who follow Western Culture, are tuned more towards Harmony rather than Melody; where as the ears of people, who follow Eastern Culture, are tuned more towards Melody rather than Harmony. Therefore, you can hear more layers of musical instruments in Western Music (e.g. Symphony Orchestra) where as you can hear more melody in the Eastern Music (e.g. Veena and Mridangam in Carnatic Music, Sitar and Tabla or Pakhawaj in Hindustani Music - One of the Melodic String Instruments and One of the Percussions). To make a huge number of musical instrument sound cohesive, we prefer to use more Harmony than Melody. If we use less musical instrument or performing a solo set, then it is better to prefer to perform Melody than Harmony.

C.V.Raman, an Indian physicist, did research that make us understand the harmonic structure of Indian musical instruments which influence the perception of pleasantness in music more as compare to Western musical instruments. He studied and explored the acoustic properties of various musical instruments, resonance patterns, sound propagation and its interaction with three dimensional surrounding environment. He recorded, observed and analysed the sound produced by various musical instruments (Tabla, Veena, Sitar, Mridangam, Violin, Piano, Drums... etc) using Fourier spectrum analysis technique and his research outcome is as follows:

Western musical instrument contains a dominant fundamental frequency with its integer multiples of harmonic overtones and produces harmonic sounds predominantly that contribute to its perceived pleasantness where as Indian musical instrument has even distribution of harmonics and contains complex harmonic structure with a range of in-harmonic overtones (that are not simple integer multiples of a fundamental frequency) and the undertones, contains distinct formant structure (frequency range at which more sound pressure levels produced), creating a unique timbre that evoke richness and beauty due to their unique construction and playing techniques using wrist, palm, fingers by the music performers. Therefore, the Indian Ragas, performed by skilful performers using traditional Indian Musical Instruments was used for healing the human body from chronic diseases.

As an Artist, Singer, Musician, Music Composer, Music Arranger or a Music Conductor, we give much more priority on our betterment of performances and quality oriented audible contents' development.

As a Sound Engineer, we give much more priority on maintaining transparency between performers and their audience or listeners technically using available tools and resources. We must know the operations of provided audio equipments and their respective signature sound based on harmonics.

As a Record Producer, Music Producer or a Music Director, Investor / Stake Holder, we give much more priority on the current trending of musical contents (events, festivals) for commercial use and business purpose.

1.3.4. Importance of Rich Contents:

Most of the songs now-a-days feels rotten and disposable type because we spend less time on rich contents' development (quality oriented audible contents' development), which results a poor content (13 points out of 90 points because of poor and unclear lyrics, poor music composition and music arrangement because of worst pitching ideas of music making by the music publisher and record producer according to their past revenue generated data sheets, poor performances of the performers because of skipping their regular practice sessions); but spend more time and money on music post-production such as editing, mixing, mastering (7 points out of 10 points).We also spend too much amount of time and money for promotion, marketing of such rotten contents.

During Music Production, we follow segment recording process(recording each artist to the same microphone(s) in the same location spot of studio space one after another).Instead of skilful musicians, most of the time we use keyboardists who use sampled musical instrument libraries and they are not able to create a natural sound of string instruments, brass instruments, woodwind instruments which a trained music programmer can do. They can't even play a musical solo piece on any one of the string instruments, brass instruments, woodwind instruments; if they try to play a musical piece on their keyboard, it will sound un-natural.

If you are a trained percussionist, you can't play a violin like a trained violinist. To play a violin like a trained violinist, you need a proper training and practice by investing a certain time and money. Similarly a trained music programmer has invested half of his/her life to learn the behaviour, the sound texture of each musical instrument using available tools and resources to produce natural sound of each instruments by listening to the masters of their respective instruments, observing the way the masters do play their instruments to convey their feelings (happy, sad, anger, aggressive…etc).A trained music programmer have attended many musical concerts, purchased many records, attended many basic lessons from each master to produce a natural sound of each instrument.

In segment recording process, a keyboardist, play almost all instruments who might be an experienced percussionist, pianist or a harmonium player but can't produce a natural sound of one of the string instruments, brass instruments, woodwind instruments. So the keyboardist's over all performance is almost zero according to evaluation process because of lack of practice his/her native instrument.

When we use skilful musicians, they can't play on tempo initially because they are habituated to focus more on producing feelings and they play at variable tempo during live performances. They are doing their jobs correctly but the amateur sound recordist always mess-up with the musicians regarding maintaining a constant tempo during recording session. Thus, the performances of all artists doesn't sound cohesive during segment recording process.

Because of evolution of technology, the singers and musicians stop or skip their practice sessions which results poor performances and the hardware equipments and software plugins have limitations to correct pitch, time and phase.

But we wonder, why the songs and musical pieces published at the end of nineteenth century have survived till now and why the record producers recreate those old songs and musical pieces which are in public domain yet !

1. Those older songs and musical pieces contain poor quality of audio (can be scored say 4 points out of 10 points) but each of them contains rich contents (can be scored say 76 points out of 90 points).A rich musical content contains a good lyrics, good music composition, good music arrangement and highly experienced musicians' performances(because of the best casting of performers, artists or musicians).Each member of the whole production team for each song had invested their valuable time in practicing and executing their respective skills.

2. Those older songs and musical pieces contain variable tempo. According to the feel of each older song and its lyrics, the tempo changes through out the song which creates interest in listening and enhance story telling experience through lyrics.

3. Before live recording, the song used to be rehearsed well and all the instruments used to be tuned well. Because of well arrangement, all the instruments sounds cohesive and create a unique product (an evergreen, gold or platinum standard song). A very huge open spaced recording venue used to be chosen for jamming, grooming, rehearsal and recording sessions. During jamming, grooming and rehearsal sessions, the available and hired cables and equipments used to be placed and routed the input and output audio signals properly, also checked for working conditions before using. If any technical problem arises related to placements of sound sources, microphones, speakers, headphones, audio and power supply equipments (absolute phase and relative phase issues, electronic noise pickups because of interference), input and output gains of the audio signals through each equipment in each audio signal chain(feedback issues), impedance matching issues of power distribution chain (affect negatively to the performance and durability of audio equipments), input and output routing of the audio signals (faulty audio cables, power cables, audio equipments...etc), audio signal processing at the input and output signal chains (dynamics issues such as masking of lead instruments because of unusual elastic properties of air medium and depth issues such as not able to represent the size of the venue), then these problems need to be resolved immediately before starting a rehearsal session.

4. After live recording, the minor editing used to be done and sent for print on LP Records, EP Records, Analog Cassette, Digital CD and other type of physical products. Limited amount of physical products results less time and money invested for promotions and marketing.

So finally an song or a musical piece published at the end of nineteenth century scores 4+76=80 points in total out of 10+90=100 points where as a rotten song (94% of songs produced now a days), scores 7+13 = 20 points in total out of 10+90=100 points.

Now-a-days you can find most of the remakes of the older songs because of a huge popularity among the audiences. It means the rich contents make a song or musical piece survive for a longer period of time.

1.3.5. Music Production Analysis:

A Dance Music is used to entertain people on the dance floor and take them on a musical journey. In dance music, the minimal instrumentation in over all arrangement allow the groove and lead vocal to stand out because of having good amount of space between them.

The verse contains soft parts of the song. In verse, the arrangement used to be minimum. The lead vocal sings very intimately and also provides dynamics.

The chorus contains loud parts of the song. The chorus section always comes after a verse section. When the chorus comes in, the synth part emphasises the chorus part and the amount of instruments are more in a chorus than a verse. In a chorus, the lead vocalist sings with more energy and volume.

A link, called as Musical Buildup, lives between a verse and chorus. It builds the climax and allows listeners to make sense of difference between the verse and the chorus.

During the making of a dance music, you will hear an abundance of vocal effects followed by a snare roll at the end of the verses. The vocal effects become louder and the snare roll speeds up. A combination of snare, kick, vocal effects increases the intensity so that the chorus intro becomes explosive.

An R&B Music uses less number of good quality of musical instruments which means we need to make the size of the music larger in the mix.

In R&B music, most accompanying instrumentation sounds softer than the lead vocal to make the music sound spacious and to make the vocals sound present. It means we keep the loudness of accompanying instruments lesser than the lead vocal.

We use shorter notes to oppose the sustained notes. The sustained instruments like electric guitar power chords, long piano drones fill up the space to contribute the loose of the song's groove coming from the kick sound.

The R&B modern music does not contain heavy instrumentation and this has an enormous effect during playback of this style of music.

For swingy and groovier beat, we delay the instruments and vocals except kick, bass and snare using available tools. It gives an impression that the kick, bass and snare are striking before anything else. That is why an R&B music always revolves around the groove.

Home Work:

Research more (to build your observation skills) about purpose, occasion, the story (through lyrics), the kind of instrumentation and instruments used in Regional Folk Music, Classical Music (both songs and instrumental music pieces), Commercials Music (Melodious type and other fusion type)

1.3.6. Skill Development in Music Performing Arts:

Singers, Musicians, Song Writers, Music Composers, Music Arrangers, Lyricists, Music Producers, Sound Production Engineers and Sound Equipment Operators including Sound Recordists, Sound Editors, Sound Mix Engineers, Sound Mastering Engineers and other team members are considered as **"Performers"** because they are the **experts** in performing their respective **arts** and **skills**.

Performance must have some **Life** that always **triggers** one of the **beautiful memories** of each listener.

Process:

1. Learn and understand the **Lyrics** (Topic, Script): Find the **Story** described in the lyrics For a better performing experiences, you can create different stories with your imaginations using the lyrics. Consider yourself as a **Lead Character** of that story who is going to express his/her **Feelings** through lyrics with a singing performance. Understand the feel of the lyrics **Word by Word** and correct your **Pronunciation** or **Phonetics**.
2. Learn & Understand the **Rhythm**.: Learn the **Taal** (Tempo) and understand the **Laya** (Time Signature) of the song.
3. Deliver your **Performance**: Find the **Key Scale** of the song and deliver your performance with correct **Pitch** (Shruti), correct **Tempo & Time Signature**

Please note that the **Time Signature** and **Pitch** are used to express **Feel** of the song

1.3.7. Sound Recording for Demo Song and Pitching:

1. At first, find a quiet place where nobody can disturb or distract you to record your song; that might be the same place

where you got ideas of writing your song or the place where you wrote your song.

2. Make sure you choose the right tempo and right scale for your song. Make sure you tuned your instruments properly to 432Hz, 417Hz or 440 Hz as a reference. Practice to put the right emotion for your lyrics before recording.

3. Record your performance using available tools with you such as a portable audio recorder, a mobile phone, tablet or personal computer with a voice recording application. Put airplane mode on your audio recording device so that your recording process won't be interrupted. If you use any MIDI sampler to trigger the pre-recorded instrument sound from the sound libraries, then you need to learn to listen well produced each instrumental records and observe each instrument's behaviour, character and try to produce the similar natural sound using velocity, pitch bend and modulation parameters available in the MIDI sampler or keyboard. A pakhawaj player cannot play a mridangam properly and cannot produce a natural sound of a mridangam; the learner need a proper training and a long period of time to practice for producing natural sound because the construction of instruments are different and the playing methods of each instrument are different to produce their respective natural sounds. A MIDI programmer always does his / her research and can produce natural sound of almost all instruments or a certain kind of instruments such as wind instruments, string instruments, brass instruments or rhythm instruments (drums and percussions).A keyboard player, who doesn't know all such informations, always produce unnatural sound of most of the instruments (violin, tuba, flute... etc) but can produce natural sound of two or three instruments (Piano, Synthesizer, bass).Similarly a MIDI guitar or sitar player always produce unnatural sound of most of the instruments (violin, tuba, flute... etc) but can produce natural sound of two or three instruments (guitar, sitar, bass).

4. Once you end your performance, wait upto 3 to 5 seconds till the sustain of your voice or your instrument fade away. Then stop your recording.

5. Name your audio files and organise with different folders depends on mood, genre, work type... etc. in two to three different storage devices including a cloud storage server. Thus you have created a bank of your assets or references for further production.

6. Go to your local recording studio and record each of your reference. You can collaborate with other artists. Name your audio files and organise with different folders depends on mood, genre, work type... etc. in two to three different storage devices and a cloud storage server.

7. To protect your work, register your songs online or offline with a Performance Rights Organisation such as ASCAP, BMI, SESAC, GEMA, SACEM, PRS, IPRS. Register yourself as a songwriter on BMI website and upload your recorded songs, BMI don't charge any fee for registration process. ASCAP charges 50 dollars, IPRS charges 1200 rupees. Add metadata (keywords) to each audio file. Have enough patience to email, research and submit your work. Improvise each of your creation to make it as a finished product. Turn the matters in your own hand and make sure that people stream your music, pay to play your music(songdew, One Music Records, Music Xray, TAXI, Broadjam...etc.) and also make sure these platforms hold up their end of bargain.

8. If you want to be independent to license your music, then there are two ways:

I) submit your songs to music production libraries driven by meta data (Songtradr, Audiosparx, DL music, Music2deal, Productiontrax, Finalcue, Indietrax, Music Dealers... etc.):

a) Meta data are the keywords through which people can find your tracks. Meta data of your song contains PRO number, admin info, genres, sub genres, reference to other tracks and other specific keywords.

b) It is advisable to sign non exclusive deals which means you as the author or owner of each of your song will get an advance money.

c) Always avoid 'race to bottom' libraries which offers least value of each of your song (20 dollar per song).

d) Reach out and update your listing regularly which means keep on making music, upload your music when finished. Send your existing music to other libraries too.

e) Experiment with your music submissions.

f) A music library works as follows:

(i) A music library create a searchable database for customers.

(ii) Customers pay synchronisation fees to the library.

(iii) As a music license provider you will get 50 percentage of the synchronisation fees.

It is great for anyone who are new to licensing but need more research to submit your audio files because you may make mistake initially in such music business and the middle man might take advantages. It is a good way to get licensing opportunities even if you have no connections.

II) Find your potential customers and sell them your products - your songs or provide your exclusive services:

a) skipping the middle man and pitch your music directly to potential customers (music supervisors, film makers, YouTubers... etc.).

b) You don't need to split your money - you keep all the money. 3) You will get more reward when you get a deal, 4) you need to work and research more on your part.

9. Meet with local producers, music lawyers, music publishers, music conductors, artist and relation people at any studio or at any venue to pitch your song or request the studio owner or studio manager to pitch your song on your behalf to the record producers, music lawyers, music publishers, music conductors and artist and relation people. Contact those people through social media and ask them what they are searching for in a song and how you can achieve it. You can pitch your song online too through social media networks and other dedicated crowdfunding websites such as Kick Starter, Wishberry, Crowd Sourcing Week

https://www.kickstarter.com
https:///www.wishberry.com
https://www.crowdsourcingweek.com

CHAPTER 2

AUDIO PRODUCTION SKILLS

Objectives:

To learn and understand

1. Listening Environment
2. Observation Skill (Listening Skill) Development
3. Difference between Rich Contents & Poor Contents
4. Rich Contents' Development
5. Different Methods of Analysing each sound

CHAPTER 2.1

SOUND RECORDING

We do Sound Recording to save useful informations so that later we can access the recorded audio file when ever required. The recorded audio might contain informations regarding education, awareness, entertainment and many more.

2.1.1. Sound Recording Process:

a) **Choosing one of the best locations** for the sound source to record: The pleasant light ambiance & good looking room may useful for video shooting & photography, but it might sound ugly and noisy.

Choose a location which sounds good for audio applications; it may be a place which looks ugly & awful, but it may sound good by controlling acoustical parameters such as

Room Shape: The room must have Non-parallel walls (to avoid existence of reflection of sound for a longer period of time) and Convex Surfaces (to scatter the sound)

Room Size: (room volume = height x breadth x length) The room dimension controls it's Resonance. It must be minimum 1500 cubic feet according to BBC which means the minimum room size will be 1971 cubic feet if height = 10feet, breadth = 12.8feet, length = 15.4feet. The recommended room dimension ratio must be

1 : 1.28 : 1.54 :: height: breadth (Width): length (Depth)

Wavelengths of the audible frequencies(20Hz to 20KHz) in air, range from about 17 meter to 17 milli meter. If you want to capture 20Hz frequency, the floor to ceiling height must be minimum 17 meters or more than 17 meters and should satisfy the room size ratio of

1 : 1.14 : 1.39	1 : 1.28 : 1.54
1 : 1.60 : 2.33	1 : 1.90 : 1.40
1 : 1.90 : 1.30	1 : 1.50 : 2.10

Similarly, the room of a home mastering studio must satisfy the ratio

1 : 1.62 :: breadth(Width): length(Depth)

To monitor and audition audio signals, the sound engineer sits at a sweet-spot of an acoustically treated room which satisfy the ratio
1 : 1.62 :: distance from sweet spot to a side wall: distance from sweet spot to a back wall
Room Isolation: Noise in the room must be less than minus 60 dB (-60dB) in your loudness measuring app or device. Outside sound must not enter in the room and sound in the room should not leak outside. Insulators such as Denim Ultra touch, Roxul materials are useful for room isolation.

Use of Acoustic Materials:

Room Acoustics always controls Reverberation Time.

Diffusers made up of Jackfruit Wood - It breaks the sound waves and converted sound energy into heat energy which can be easily absorbed by nearby absorbing materials. Alternative of diffusers can be books arranged in longer deep book shelves, clothes in your longer deep wardrobe.

Reflectors - It reflect pleasant frequencies. Reflectors are made up of pure metals or a combination of metals.

Absorbers - It absorbs the converted heat energy of unpleasant and unwanted frequencies. Most of the radio stations and sound recording studios use the concept of Helmholtz resonator for sound absorption. Walls made of plaster of paris, having a number of small holes, used to install on the 9" to16" thick hard surfaced walls. The air gape between hard surfaced wall and installed plaster of paris wall absorbs the converted heat energy. The size of the hole is determined by a quarter of wave length of unpleasant and unwanted frequency(wavelength divided by 4).

(Glass wool)   (Rock wool)

In general, the absorbers are having dimensions 4 feet x 2 feet x 4 inch (thickness varies from 2 inches to 6 inches). To absorb mid and high frequencies, we use a combination of a rock wool slab and a glass wool slab in an MDF wooden panel (having thickness of 22mm). To absorb low frequencies, we use a combination of a geo wool slab(3rd layer at back side), a glass wool slab (2nd layer, sandwiched between geo wool and rock wool) and a rock wool slab (1st layer at front side) in a Medium-density Fibreboard (MDF) wooden panel having thickness of 22mm. So, the wooden panel's inner dimension could be 4'5" x 2'5" x 8'5". You can follow a DIY approach by taking 7 to 8 numbers of thick blankets, having good absorption quality of materials, sewed together to make it look more thick around 6 to 8 inches can be used as absorbers.

(MDF wooden panel having thickness of 22mm)

Note: Damping Factor of a selected location will be great, if Room Shape, Room Size, Room Isolation, right choice of acoustic materials (if required) for the selected location, design of the location and solid materials used to build the location are great with proper air conditioning having say, 16 degree to 22 degree of air temperature (less room temperature results more air density which provide great damping of air medium and great performance delivery of the performers) of the selected location. Because the Room of recording studio or chosen outdoor location is an important part of sound while recording a sound source. Poor damping factor of a location means wrong choice of location for sound recording.

Properties of Acoustical Environment:

Attenuation of certain frequencies occurs due to Humidity, Density, Temperature and other related factors of Air Medium. The Reflection and Diffraction of sound always occurs around Solid Objects. Refraction and shadow formation of frequencies occurs due to change in Air Temperature and effect of Wind. The Reflections and Absorptions happens by Earth's surface itself. Reverberation is a result of Multiple Simultaneous Reflection created from all room surfaces. Intensity and Duration of reverberation depends on Room's Dimensions and Absorption Characteristics of the surfaces. Reverberation Time is the time taken for Reverb to die away (sound energy of reverb diffuses and converts into heat energy) by dropping to 60 decibel of Sound Pressure Level of Reverb. Reverberation Time is always measured using 1KHz tone.

b) **Choosing microphones** (input transducers) for each sound source: The bass sound source travels omni-directionally i.e, equal distance to all directions from the sound source. The treble sound source travels much more directional than bass sound source by shifting more energy from the sides to front & back.

Thus polar pattern of the microphone are designed as follows:
Sub-cardioid: It captures a sound more from the sides but less from the front. It doesn't capture sound from rear side of the microphone.

It is used to capture bass (low frequency) sound source such as Kick sound of a drum kit.

Cardioid: It captures a sound more from the front but less from the sides. It rejects sound from the back. It is used to capture mid frequency sound source such a vocal recording for Music Production, Podcasting... etc.

Hyper Cardioid and Super Cardioid: They capture a sound from a larger distance at front side more than back side but will not capture from the sides because of cancelling the sounds from the sides. Both kind of polar patterns are used to capture the sound source that produce upper-mid frequency sounds and treble sound(high frequency). They are popularly used for on-location recording in a noisy environment such as interview session of news channels and television channels at an outdoor location, dialog recording of actors at an outdoor location for film, television and video streaming service providers. The pickup patterns of microphones are as follows:

Omni-directional - To capture Low Frequency sound sources
Uni-directional - To capture Mid Frequency sound sources
Bi-Directional - To capture High Frequency sound sources

Because high frequencies travel more front and back directions quickly than low frequencies and mid frequencies if there is no barrier to stop or diverge their directions.

Choosing microphones also balance the harmonics of all sounds that we hear collectively during recording process or after recording process. The microphones could be tube based (for introducing even harmonics) or transistor based (for introducing odd harmonics).

Types of Microphones (Input Transducers):

Moving Coil Microphones	Ribbon Microphones	Condenser Microphones
Based on Electro Magnetic Induction Principle	Based on Electro Magnetic Induction Principle	Based on Electro Static Principle
Insensitive to change in humidity & temperature	Insensitive to change in humidity & temperature	More sensitive to change in humidity & temperature
Robust & Durable	Fragile	More Fragile
Inexpensive	Expensive	Very Expensive
Uni and omni directional pickup patten by default	Bi directional pickup pattens by default	Omni directional pickup pattens by default
Because of more impedance and less sensitivity, it captures sounds from less area of coverage. It is used for capturing louder sounds.	Because of moderate impedance and moderate sensitivity, it captures sounds from a decent area of coverage because of good quality of transformer used. It is used for capturing louder sounds and high frequency sounds.	Because of less impedance and more sensitivity, it captures sounds from more area of coverage. It is used for capturing softer sounds and reflected sounds (room sounds).
More mass of the diaphragm results weak High Frequency response	Moderate mass of the diaphragm results balanced frequency response	Less mass of the diaphragm results weak Low Frequency response

Note: If we put a ribbon microphone in an angular position by tilting it after its positioning near the sound source, then a 3dB boost at around 10 KHz happens due to gravity.

To record a line source such as Drums and Percussion instruments, the similar model of microphones are used for stereo recording. To record a point source such as Lead Vocal and other Lead instruments, different model of microphones are used.

According to the technology developed in manufacturing audio equipments, the dis-advantages mentioned above has been over-come; such as

1. Dynamic microphones has enough high frequency response because of making the diaphragm thin and light weight by weaving different kind of conducting materials resulting less impedance.
2. We can use +48 Volt phantom power to make bidirectional polar pattern to unidirectional of a few Ribbon Microphone manufacturers.
3. Condenser microphones having uni-directional polar pattern, less sensitivity are not expensive now-a-days and can also operated at room temperature

Fill in the blanks:

Properties of Sound Source   Properties of Microphone

Frequency Response	Loudness (Overall SPL)	ADSR Info	Example of Sound Source	Type of Microphone	Polar Pattern	Example of Microphone
HF	Louder	Transient	Close Hihat	Dynamic with thin Diaphragm	Hyper Cardioid	Audix OM2
HF	Louder	Sustain	Cymbal, Ride	Dynamic with thin Diaphragm	Hyper Cardioid	
HF	Softer	Transient	Shaker	Condenser & Ribbon	Hyper Cardioid	
HF	Softer	Sustain	Chymes	Condenser & Ribbon	Hyper Cardioid	
MF	Louder	Transient	Snare	Dynamic	Cardioid	Shure SM57

Frequency Response	Loudness (Overall SPL)	ADSR Info	Example of Sound Source	Type of Microphone	Polar Pattern	Example of Microphone
MF	Louder	Sustain	Electric Gtr Amp	Dynamic	Cardioid	Shure SM58, Audix OM3
MF	Softer	Transient	Vocals	Condenser & Ribbon	Cardioid	
MF	Softer	Sustain	Acoustic Guitar, Violin	Condenser & Ribbon	Cardioid	
LF	Louder	Transient	Kick	Dynamic with thick Diaphragm	Sub-cardioid	
LF	Louder	Sustain	Bass Amp	Dynamic	Sub-cardioid	
LF	Softer	Transient	Floor Tom	Condenser Ribbon	Omni Cardioid or Sub-cardioid	
LF	Softer	Sustain	Double Bass	Condenser Ribbon	Omni (for condenser) Cardioid or Sub-cardioid (for Ribbon)	

Note: If you want to increase sensitivity (area of coverage from which a microphone takes the sound as an input) of a microphone, increase input gain by increasing trim knob or gain knob at your microphone preamplifier.

c) **Finding sweet spots for placing microphones and sound sources** at the chosen location - more noise controlled, more isolated spot for each sound source and microphone placement.

Finding right kind of distance (for both close miking and distant miking) by fixing the mic placement and moving the sound source on axis (only relative phase issue exists which can be solved easily using audio editing process) and off axis (absolute phase & relative phase issues exist from which absolute phase issue can't be solved easily using audio editing process)

a) Distance for Close Miking is around 3 c.m.
b) Distance for Mid Miking is between 15 c.m. to 30 c.m.
c) Distance for Distant Miking is more than 75 c.m.

Note: Audio Signal Processors are used for two purposes:

1. Audio Signal Processing - Popularly used by the users
2. Monitoring the Audio Signals - Rarely used by the users but popularly used by Audio Professionals during audio recording, audio editing, mixing and mastering.

Therefore, while recording an artist, editing and mixing by yourself or playback your work to your clients, use a low-level compressor/limiter as a magnifying glass to monitor your surgical work. Once you completed your work, bypass or disconnect safely the signal processors that are used for monitoring (such as low-level compressor/limiter) before exporting your audio tracks. In this way, you can maintain a decent amount of headroom for your exported tracks.

For close miking, a louder sound source need more distance from the microphone where as a softer sound source need less distance from the microphone. But to understand how much distance, we need to isolate our right ear with an earplug and use our left ear as a microphone and place our left ear near the active sound source to discover a good sounding spot and replace your left ear from that discovered good sounding spot with the microphone chosen. It is important to maintain 3:1 ratio of Distant Miking Distance (3 units) vs Close Miking Distance (1 unit).

Sound travels at a speed of 1130 feet per seconds (344 meters per second) approximately which means for 1 millisecond (0.001 second) time delay, we need to set the distance 1.130 foot (34.4 centimeters or 0.344 meter).

For point sources, mono miking techniques are recommended where as for line sources, stereo miking techniques are recommended. If we record a line source using mono miking technique, then the recorded sound used to be considered as the sound captured from a point source.

Note: Before connecting equipments using audio cables with each other, make sure their power switch is off and also make sure each equipment's output gain is set to zero. After connecting the audio cables among the audio equipments, connect the power cables of each equipment for power supply (3 phase power supply is recommended for using mixing console far field monitors and audio signal processing units in the rack mounts). Once again make sure each audio equipment's output gain is set to minimum available and the power switch of each audio equipments are off.

Once connections are done, then you can start boot up process(switching on the power supply of the equipments from the output of your audio signal chain onwards: At first, turn the power on of the speakers or speaker amplifiers, then turn the output gain of each speaker up to 50%(12 O' clock, upto 0 dB loudness indication) and at last, turn on the power of the microphones' pre-amplifiers or mixer or audio interface, then turn the input gain of each microphone's pre-amplifier up to 25%(position - upto 9 O' clock) for less impedance condenser microphone, 75%(position - upto 3 O' clock) for high impedance moving coil microphones).

If we have connected the microphone to a Magnetic Tape Recorder, then we operate it on Repro mode and use the following method:

1. Increase Bias (increase input knob, decrease output knob if Bias is not available) for Softer Sustained sounds (e.g:- Violin, Bass Guitar)
2. Decrease Bias (decrease input knob, increase output knob if Bias is not available) for Louder Transient sounds (e.g:- Kick Drum, Close Hi-hat)

3. Use 15 IPS (inch per second) or Higher Magnetic Tape Speed and NAB Repro EQ for Low Frequency Sounds (e.g:- Kick Drum, Bass Guitar)
4. Use 7.5 IPS (inch per second) or Lower Magnetic Tape Speed and CCIR Repro EQ for High Frequency Sounds (e.g:- Violin, Close Hi-hat)

For a Kick Drum, we apply less Bias with NAB Repro EQ at the rate of higher Magnetic Tape Speed (15 IPS)

For a Bass Guitar, we apply more Bias with NAB Repro EQ at the rate of higher Magnetic Tape Speed (15 IPS)

For a Closed Hi-hat, we apply less Bias with CCIR Repro EQ at the rate of slower Magnetic Tape Speed (7.5 IPS)

For a Violin, we apply more Bias with CCIR Repro EQ at the rate of slower Magnetic Tape Speed (7.5 IPS)

Once your work (Recording, Editing, Mixing, Mastering) is done, you need to follow the boot down process (reverse process of boot up process - switching off the power supply of the equipments from the input of your audio signal chain onwards: At first, turn the input gain(trim) up to minimum available of the mic pre-amplifiers or mixer or audio interface and turn the power off of the microphones' pre-amplifiers or mixer or audio interface. At last, turn the output gain of speakers or speaker amplifiers up to minimum available and turn the power off of the speakers or speaker amplifiers).

2.1.2. Analysis of 3D space environment around sound sources:

The study of Auditory Sensation is known as Acoustics and the Perception of Sound Waves by our ear is known as Psychoacoustics. Our human brain process the Time Difference and Intensity Difference between our two ears indicate it's Direction, Location and Distance.

If you imagine a performing stage as a listener,

1. the X-Axis indicates Panaroma parameter or sound source placement for Width (Locating the sound left side or right side) which can be implemented by Sound Source & Microphone placements at Left, Centre, or Right side of the stage using Mono Miking, Stereo Miking and Surround Miking techniques.
2. the Y-Axis indicates Frequency parameter for height (putting bass sound on the floor, treble sound at the ceiling) which can be implemented by Choosing the right kind of microphones for each sound source.
3. the Z-Axis indicates Dynamics (difference between louder and softer sound or change in elastic property of air medium during compression and rarefaction or change in Amplitude of the audible sound between near and far placements of a sound source) & Depth (sound response of the environment or

reflected sound of the environment) which can be implemented by Maintaining a proper distance from each sound source to all the microphones i.e. putting the sound source near to the listener (more dynamics of sound with less reflection sound) or far from the listener (less dynamics of sound with more reflection sound).

CHAPTER 2.2

SOUND EDITING

We do scrap the existing unwanted audio clips(regions) by editing the recorded audio file.

Tools used for Editing Analog Tapes:

A Pencil or Marker Tool is used to mark the unwanted parts of the tape.
A Scissor Tool is popularly used to

1. scrap the unwanted sound materials of the tape
2. cut (trim) and join the tapes
3. fade-in and fade-out the sound in the tapes

A certain kind of paste is used to join the needed parts of the tape reels.
Tools used for Editing in Digital Audio Editor of a Digital Audio Work Station:
The tools' pallet in the audio editor is called as Tool Bar. In the Tool Bar, we have

1. Marque Tool to mark the unwanted parts of the digital sound track (Audio Track and MIDI Track).

2. Scissor Tool to cut and scrap the unwanted sound materials of the recorded digital sound track (Audio Track and MIDI Track).

3. Fade Tool to fading in and fading out the sound in the used portions (known as Regions or Clips) of the digital sound track (Audio Track and MIDI Track).

4. Hand Tool used to move the Regions (Clips).

5. Trim Tool used to open the beginning and ending portions of a Region (Clip) of a digital sound track or trim the beginning and ending portions of a Region (Clip).

6. Gain Tool to increase or decrease the loudness of Regions or Clips.

7. Automation Tool to automate the parameters such as loudness, panning …etc of a digital sound track (Audio Track and MIDI Track).

8. Pencil Tool to create an empty region (empty clip) in the Edit Window (Arrange Window); also used to create notes in the MIDI Editor; also used to create automation curves of the assigned parameters of an audio and an MIDI track in the Edit (Arrange) Window and in the MIDI Editor.

2.2.1. Setting up a session for Audio Editing:

1. Create a new session in your digital audio work station. Setup Sample Rate, Bit Depth, Tempo, Time Signature, Key Scale and save your session in an organised location which contains a proper file management system.

2. Always communicate and keep in touch with the Sound Recordist and document the informations regarding audio equipments used in audio recording, places of audio recording, process of recording, the problems resolved by Sound Recordist and the problems to be resolved by Mix Engineer… etc. Import your audio tracks in your work station, rename them, colour code them; then you start your work.

2.2.2. Audio Editing Process:

1. Import a well produced and mastered song for your loudness reference. Once the loudness is set, do a rough balance of your recorded audio files on audio tracks in mono (panning the tracks to one of the speakers) using available gain tools of the regions/clips or inserting a gain tool at each track instead of using linear faders of the tracks at mix window. Before editing by yourself, you can use a low-level compressor/limiter as a magnifying glass to monitor your surgical work at the master bus.

2. At first, identify transients of the recorded file to identify tempo. Do tempo mapping with time signature if recorded live for the ease of audio editing. If you are a songwriter and produce your own song, then do tempo mapping to replace a boring constant tempo to an interesting variable tempo according to the feel of the song. For a demanding creative work, you can also transform the imported mastered audio files and audio loops by pitch matching and tempo matching to your project's key scale and project's tempo respectively which is also a useful trick while using audio loops for your music production.

3. Clean up the tracks by removing clicks, pops and other unwanted noises. At input of a tape recorder, sometimes it is better to increase bias to recover transients of the sound or decrease bias to remove transients of the sound during recording process. At the output of a tape recorder, it is better to increase lower frequencies to make the sound thicker during playback of the sound of that audio. In short, we increase the loudness of the harmonics of that sound which feels pleasant to human ears.

4. Balance the loudness of regions (clips) of each track - Find Louder parts, Softer parts, Nominal Level (Average Audible Level) areas of each portion of the song (Intro, Verse, Pre-Chorus, Chorus, Bridge, Outro) by listening each track and

also listening to the context(overall sound) to decide whether it sounds balanced with other instruments or not, mark and name them using markers, decrease the louder parts upto the nominal level of each portion (Intro, Verse, Pre-Chorus, Chorus, Bridge, Outro) by listening, increase the softer parts upto the nominal level of each portion (Intro, Verse, Pre-Chorus, Chorus, Bridge, Outro) by listening which are not clearly audible. Always try to build the dynamics of a song (e.g:-The verse contains soft parts of the song. In verse, the arrangement used to be minimum. The lead vocal sings very intimately and also provides dynamics. The chorus contains loud parts of the song. The chorus section always comes after a verse section.)

5. Time Correction - We take lead instruments (e.g:- lead vocals) as reference and solve Relative Phase issue of other audio tracks by compensating Time Delay by dragging the regions or tracks. We can also solve Absolute Phase issue by reversing its phase at the insert or at the channel.

6. Pitch Correction - We can correct the pitch by Semitones and Cents.

7. Waveform Alignment - We can re-verify the solution of absolute phase issues, relative phase issues and time alignment issues of similar instruments such as Lead Vocals with Backing Vocals, Lead String Instruments with Backing String Instruments (by taking lead string instruments as a reference), Lead Percussion Instruments (e.g:- a Tabla) with Backing Percussion Instruments (e.g:- a Manjira)

8. Use of Filters - Remove the unwanted overtones and unwanted harmonics of each sound track using Low Pass Filter and High Pass Filter

9. Once you completed audio editing process, bypass or disconnect the signal processors safely that are used for monitoring (limiter and/or low-level compressor) before exporting your audio tracks.

Note:- Put the play head at a region/clip and zoom in to make visible of waveforms and their respective zero crossing points. Always cut at zero crossing point of a waveform during time correction, pitch correction and waveform alignment.

2.2.3. Radio Edit for Audio Applications such as Radio, AM/FM Stations, Disc Jockeys

1. In this case, you, as an audio editor, may be instructed to shortened a musical piece or a song as per requested time durations by the client.e.g:- 3 minute time duration of a musical piece or song need to be shortened and the client might ask 3,10,15,30,45,60,90,120,150 seconds of edits according to the time slots available for broadcasting.

2. The edit can be done without finding tempo by cutting the required portions from the kick hit to kick hit transients of the song or audio file. The edit can also be done after tempo mapping by cutting the required portions from bar to bar of each song or audio file. e.g:- After finding the right tempo, say 25th bar to 36th bar of a song is the required portion to be used. At 25th bar and 36th bar kick hits will be present, Similarly say 49th bar to 52nd bar of the same song can be edited, if it is a needful portion. You can cut any portion of the song if that sound completed such as any verse portion of the song you can cut to use, any chorus portion of the song you can use. Similarly you can cut intro, bridge, outro portions and shuffle them to re-arrange for new edits.

3. To shorten a musical piece, you need to assemble the chosen portions, shuffle the portions.e.g:- the chosen portions could be intro, 1st verse, 2nd chorus and outro and arrange those portions as per your need, such as intro-2nd chorus-outro.

4. To make your edit sound smooth, musical, you need to place the 2nd chorus after the intro properly. To make it happen, select intro portion and find the first kick hit of the first verse by opening the intro portion temporarily for kick hit

reference. Then, place the 2nd chorus portion on the top of opening section of intro portion in such a way that the first kick hit of 2nd chorus portion will sit exactly on the top of the first kick hit of the first verse of the opened intro portion through waveform alignment of both kick hit transients that aligns their zero crossing points. You can also do waveform alignment using two different tracks and trim the unwanted areas of the regions/clips at their respective zero crossing points.

5. After the proper assembling of intro and 2nd chorus portions, put a cross fade between them for smoothness if zero crossing points are not available or you can arrange those portions in different tracks, put fade-in fade-out of each portion and automate the pan of the fade in portion to left side around 11 O' clock and automate the pan of the fade-out portion to right-side around 2 O' clock during Radio Edit if required. Similarly, assemble the outro portion as described above. Thus you got your first radio edit: intro-2nd chorus-outro. Then you can export your radio edit.

6. As your client needs multiple edits of the available time slots for them to broadcast their audio visual advertisement, you need to prepare 2 to 3 options of each time duration edits for your backup. If your client didn't like or reject your 30 second edit, ask them for a feedback. Though you have 2 or 3 options of 30 second edit, you can do minor changes as per client's feedback and email a draft of the 30 second edit options to your client with a non-disclosure clause notification to remind him/her about the contract agreement.

2.2.4. Radio Edit for Audio-visuals such as Television Shows, Ad Films, Movies

1. During Radio Edit or preparing edit for a showreel, you, as an audio editor, may get multiple number of audio files or

songs (e.g:- 6 songs). At first, you need to import all musical pieces or songs.

2. It is recommended to cut the needful portions(Intro, Verse, Pre-Chorus, Chorus, Bridge, Outro) of each song from kick hit to kick hit that starts and end at their respective zero crossing points. Name the chosen portions (newly created regions/clips) according to their role in the radio edit such as intro, verse, pre-chorus, chorus, bridge and outro.

3. Then, arrange those renamed chosen portions (newly created regions/clips) according to their relative pitch. In Indian music, Sa, Ga, Pa are the relative pitches to one another. So take one of the portions as your reference in such a way that its relative pitches matches to more number of selected portions. You need to arrange the relative pitch based audio clips/regions next to each other and re arrange again from lower pitch to higher pitch or slower tempo to faster tempo. The non-relative portions can be arranged before and/or after the relative portion edits in such a way that the radio edit need to sound cohesive like a complete song containing intro, verse, pre-chorus, chorus, bridge and outro. For a demanding creative work, you can also transform the imported mastered audio files by pitch matching and tempo matching to your project's key scale and project's tempo respectively or considering one of the audio track as a reference which is also a useful trick while using audio loops for your music production.

4. The assembling of selected portions can be done by matching the kick hits technique as described in 'Radio Edit for Audio Applications'.After that, arrange each portions in different tracks without changing their respective placements by duplicating the current track 6 times, if number of chosen portions are 6.Name those duplicate tracks as intro, verse, pre-chorus, chorus, bridge and outro. Then delete unwanted duplicated chosen portions that doesn't match the track name. It means, at intro track, intro portion only will be there.

5. You need to match the loudness of each selected portion by taking a soft sounding musical portion as a reference and decrease the loudness of other musical portions to have equal loudness in the radio edit.

6. After the proper assembling of chosen portions in different tracks, put fade-in fade-out of each portion and pan the fade-in portion to left side around 11 O' clock to automate 11 O' clock left to centre and pan the fade-out portion to right-side around 2 O' clock to automate centre to 2 O' clock right during Radio Edit using automation process if required. Then you can export your radio edit.

7. As your client needs multiple edits of the available time slots for them to broadcast their audio visual advertisement, you need to prepare 2 to 3 options of each time duration edits for your backup. If your client didn't like or reject your 30 second edit, ask them for a feedback.

8. Though you have 2 or 3 options of 30 second edit, you can do minor changes as per client's feedback and email a draft of the 30 second edit options to your client with a non-disclosure clause notification to remind him/her about the contract agreement.

2.2.5. Background Scoring Process for Audio Visuals:

1. Create a blank session in your digital audio workstation with the following settings: 24 bit Bitdepth, 48 KHz Samplerate, 24 fps, enable or add immersive sound feature

2. Import the audio visual clip (mov file format to import individual tracks such as dialogues, foley sound, reference background music...etc) to your digital audio work station

3. Import the audio files to your digital audio work station by extracting the audio from the audio visual clip. Use the imported audio files as it is. Please note not to edit, automate or do any audio signal processing of the audio files extracted from the movie.

4. Cross check the audio tracks whether it synchronise to the visual or not and rename the tracks according to the file management system that you follow.

5. Collect as much data as possible about the movie from the scripts, news, blogs, vlogs, social-media and other media available.

6. Watch the movie and note down the feel of the story divided into different themes of the audio visual. Name each theme with different Ragas according to the feel of the story section because each Raga indicates different feelings such as love, anger, horror... etc

7. Find the rhythm of the audio visual. If required, automate the tempo and time signature with click according to the 'change of shots' of each time frame or follow 'the rhythm of visible activities' in the visual that provides a cue for tempo automation.

   Set up tempo and time signature for each time length according to the frame change, action or movement of each subject or object of the audio-visual (e.g:- Faster Tempo for a fight scene because of faster frame change or action or movement of each subject or object in the fight scene. Here the goal is to make the tempo of background music fit and synchronise with the visual).

8. For scoring a longer length of audio-visual, divide the whole time length of audio-visual into shorter time periods (varies from 1 minute to 10 minutes) and add names and descriptions (musical descriptions) according to the feel of story for each time period (for which you are going to make Background Scores and put Foley Sounds and Dialogues).

   Watch the full audio-visual (Ad Film, Movie Reel) and document the time period to put Foley Sounds and Background Scores.

   Start your music scoring task. Once your music score is finalised, verified and completed, then start music programming. After finishing the music programming, then finalise, verify and complete the sound recording of the music performers. Re-record the dialogues and foley sounds according to the tempo, time signature and description if necessary.

9. Mute the audio in the audio visual clip at the audio visual project settings in your digital audio workstation before exporting your music to the audiovisual clip

10. After finishing music score, export your music to the audiovisual clip

Note:

Pitch up or down an instrument and transpose it back to its original notes allows to play different samples at the same pitch in order to create a richer and wider sound

Pitch and transpose up or down - pitch down 2 layers, pitch up 1 layer will provide 4 layer using 1 instrument that save tons of cpu memory or to get rid of cpu overload issue. e.g:- values to be pitched up or down to achieve 4 layers could be -7, -4, 0, +4

Then automate the loudness or volume parameter to add more dynamics after finishing your music programming.

Here, the whole idea of learning Sound Editing is to focus on career objectives such as Music Arranger, Music Supervisor, Remixer, Sound Editor. Once you become an expert in Sound Editing by practicing regularly and pursuing career objective as Music Arranger, Music Supervisor, Remixer, Sound Editor, then you can start assisting a Music Producer or a Mix Engineer to learn more about Audio Signal Processing Methods and create a case study report about the learnt methods.

Homework:

1. Create Sound Sample Libraries for Musical Instrument, Foley Sound, Impulse Responses and Musical Loops using sound editing techniques

2. Create Master Edits using provided audio files for the purpose of Music Showreel Creation, Radio Edits based on provided time lengths (available time slots), Master Edit including replacement of Re-recorded Sound (Replacing the performance of one artist with a new one)

2.2.6. Premix / Music Arranging / Music Remix:

Before we take a picture / photo using a camera, we focus on an object and give more space to occupy in the frame where as the background objects or views become blurred so that the focused object will stand out because the focused object contain much more important informations or memory of that moment for you than the background objects or views. When everything is sorted, we click to capture that moment.

Similarly, we focus on the lead instruments during editing. Because the lead singer sings the lyrics or the lead actor speaks the dialogue which is an important information or a story to consume. The foley sounds give more information of the surrounding environment of the lead actors or lead singers and their activities.

The rhythm instruments such as rhythm guitar, piano, drum kit and percussions take care of the tempo to support the lead instruments. The bass sustained lead instruments such as double bass or bass guitar represents the body and energy of the song. Other sustained instruments such as electronic synth, synth pad, string ensemble, brass ensemble, woodwind ensemble supports the lead instruments to fill the empty spaces.

So we edit the lead musical instruments (e.g:- lead vocals) or the dialogues at first and provide them enough space, enough size, enough body by providing a decent loudness, taking off unwanted frequencies using filters, add the room mic signals, that capture the surrounding informations of lead musical instruments (e.g:- lead vocal for a song; veena, sitar, flute, violin...etc for an instrumental music piece), by compensating their loudness and frequencies as per required. Once you are happy with your mixed sound of your lead instrument or lead dialogue, then you can proceed editing of supporting instruments, foley sounds (if any) and compensate their loudness and frequencies comparing with lead instruments so that all the elements and parameters of the instruments will fit in your rough mix. If you haven't recorded the room sound using a pair of identical room mics, then you have an option to pan the closely miked musical instruments at their respective channel-strip and add a digital delay (1 foot = 0.9 milli second in air medium) with a convolution reverb (that process through the captured impulse response signals of an acoustically reflected chambers) to create a virtual space or a virtual room at an auxiliary channel and send each instrument's signal from its channel to the auxiliary channel as per your taste or flavour just like the way your mother cook your favourite dish. The amount of sending the signals from each instrument to the virtually created room as per your taste is just like how much pepper, how much salt, how much vinegar, how much jaggery to add, collectively gives a signature flavour of home cooked dish that you love. Once we are happy with such rough mix, we export dry signals of each instrument separately, wet signals (processed signals) of each instruments separately and submit all those audio tracks to the studio server followed by a file management system for further audio signal processing. As per assigned by Chief Mix Engineer, we do audio signal routing and re-routing to optimise the size of data and number of audio tracks. Because, an audio console used to have 48 tracks where as the audio content creator (Music Composer, Music Programmer, Music Performer, Record Producer) might provide you more than 100 tracks.

CHAPTER 2.3

SOUND MIXING

You don't need to go through the process of sound mixing, if you did sound recording properly. If you did sound recording in a worse sounding location or wrong acoustic treatment of the location (contains wrong room size, wrong room dimension, wrong room isolation if done or no room isolation, wrong use of acoustic materials for absorption, reflection, diffusion, or no use of acoustic materials to control the sound reflection resulting poor damping factor of the room), we shouldn't even think about sound mixing; it is recommended to redo the sound recording in a good sounding location (e.g:- Recording Studios, Concert Venues... etc).

Still if you try to bring a good sound which is recorded at worse sounding location, by applying the recommended mixing process, the result will be more worse and awful. Therefore, it is recommended to spend more money and time in Acoustical Treatment of a good sounding room instead of spending more money on purchasing audio hardware equipments and softwares or other related tools and accessories. We don't guarantee that all the problems can be solved by the audio equipments. Because the audio hardware equipments and softwares, we use, has a limitation to serve you.

"It is difficult to bring a good taste out of rotten vegetables."

You need sound mixing process if the following problem exists during sound recording:

1. If choosing of microphones for each sound source is not correct or used available microphones to record each sound source that is happening now-a-days.
2. If microphone placement for each sound source in the recorded location is not correct which might arise phase issues
3. If sound source placement in the recorded location is not correct (if distance among the microphones to each sound source is not correct)

The solution of such problems during sound recording can be as follows:

1. Use equaliser tool or hardware, if the choosing of microphones for each sound source is not quite right or used available microphones to record the sound.
2. Use panorama potentiometer (pan-pot in short) for width control of a stereo image, if microphone placement for each sound source in the recorded location is not correct (might result absolute phase issues and/or relative phase issues).
3. Use dynamic processing tools (Expander for upward expansion, Compressor and Limiter for downward compression, Noise Gate for downward expansion, Digital Compressor for upward compression or low level compression) and time based processing tools (use of delay for reverb and echo effect) to place each sound source correctly in the location, if distance between each microphone to each sound source is not properly made.
4. Use gain tool or input trim tool to resolve loudness issues. Balance the loudness of regions (clips) of each track - Find Louder parts, Softer parts, Nominal Level (Average Audible Level) areas of each portion of the song (Intro, Verse, Pre-Chorus, Chorus, Bridge, Outro) by listening each track and compare it by listening to the context(overall sound) to decide whether it sounds balanced with other instruments or not, mark and name them using markers, decrease the louder

parts upto the nominal level of each portion (Intro, Verse, Pre-Chorus, Chorus, Bridge, Outro) by listening, increase the softer parts upto the nominal level of each portion (Intro, Verse, Pre-Chorus, Chorus, Bridge, Outro) by listening which are not clearly audible as comparing it by listening to the context(overall sound).Always try to build the dynamics of a song (e.g:-The verse contains soft parts of the song. In verse, the arrangement used to be minimum. The lead vocal sings very intimately and also provides dynamics. The chorus contains loud parts of the song. In a chorus, the lead vocal sings with more energy that sounds louder.)

Note: To make the sound of background music or supporting instruments (such as background choir) coming from a larger distance,

(i) we choose a dedicated microphone for a certain sound source.
(ii) we reduce dynamic range of the sound and add an information about the size of the chosen location by placing a microphone at a larger distance from the sound source which is preferred and recommended by well experienced and skilful sound engineers.

— OR —

a) we cut the mid frequency range using a band-stop filter,
b) we reduce dynamic range of the sound by using fast attack (less attack time) and fast release (less release time) setting in a compressor; where as for individual sound sources, we manipulate dynamic range of the sound by using attack and release parameters according to the envelope of each sound source at the input to the compressor used.
c) we add a reflected sound of the room by processing through an impulse response of a location using a convolution reverb (that add information about the size of chosen location).

Note that the signal processors (both hardware and analog emulated plugins) has a limitation to do signal processing. Most of the Recording Engineers, Mix Engineers and Mastering Engineers prefer Analog Work Station (a combination of analog tape recorders, an analog mix desk and analog signal processors) or a Hybrid Work Station (a combination of a Digitally Recorded Players or a computer system having a Digital Audio Work Station, an analog mix desk and analog signal processors) to begin their work.

Always communicate and keep in touch with the Sound Recordist and Sound Editor and document the informations regarding audio equipments used in recording, editing, places of recording and editing, process of recording and editing, the problems resolved by Sound Recordist and Sound Editor and the problems to be resolved by Mix Engineer... etc. Import your audio tracks in your work station, rename them, save the project according to your file management system, colour code them; then you start your work on mixing.

2.3.1. Audio Signal Processors

Role of Audio Signal Processors:

Audio Signal Processors are used for two purposes:

1. Monitoring the Audio Signals - Rarely used by the users but popularly used by Audio Professionals
2. Audio Signal Processing (if incorrect microphone choices and their incorrect mic placements exist) - Popularly used by the users

Fab Filter, Harrison Consoles, Klanghelm, Plugin Alliance, Shatter Glass Audio, Softtube, Tokyo Dawn Labs, Sonnox, Brainworx, Universal Audio, Valhalla DSP LLC, Vladislav Goncharov, Townsend Labs, Tdrl, TDR Labs, GPU Audio and many more are the manufacturers of Audio Signal Processors in plugin formats.

Note: The **lead instruments** during **slower tempo** and **supporting instruments** during **faster tempo** need to be processed with **tube** based audio signal processors for **even harmonics** processing where as **lead instruments** during **faster tempo** and **supporting instruments** during **slower tempo** need to be processed with **transistor** and **diode** based audio signal processors for **odd harmonics** processing.

Get as more informations as possible from the Sound Editor, Sound Recordist, Record Producer (Music Director) and client about recording process, editing process and their individual DAW session informations and note them immediately. At first prepare a session on your DAW by finalising Tempo, Time-signature, Key scale, Sample-rate, Bit-depth ...etc. After preparing your session for mixing, import the audio files. Rename and colour-code the audio tracks.

The mixing and mastering techniques, described below, might or might not be useful according to your workflow in your DAW; but try them once. If you like any processes and make you feel useful for your workflow, then you can adapt those selected processes and include them in your workflow.

2.3.2. Introduction to Audio Signal Processors:

2.3.2.1. *Distortion:*

It is also known as Harmoniser, Exciter, Saturator, Drive.

Types of Distortion:

1. Tube and analog tape distortion circuits introduce even harmonics (e.g.:- 200Hz, 400Hz, 800Hz... and so on) and contain more impedance values. Such distortion sounds smoother and rounder. Products belong to Neve, Harrison, Studer, Ampex companies provide even harmonics distortions. Blues, Jazz, Classical contain more sustained instruments that prefer even harmonics distortions. The energy / power supplied to a high impedance circuit can drive low frequencies

very easily but the mid and high frequencies get absorbed by the circuit itself as compared to low frequencies. As a result, the output of the high impedance circuit sound warm and dull.

2. Transistors and Operational Amplifier circuits always introduce odd harmonics (e.g.:- 100Hz, 300Hz, 500Hz… and so on) contain less impedance values. Such distortion sounds buzzier. Products belong to SSL, API companies provides odd harmonics distortions. Pop, Rock Music contains less sustained instruments (transient instruments) that prefer odd harmonics distortion. The energy / power supplied to a low impedance circuit can't drive low frequencies. To drive low frequencies, we need more power but if we provide more power to the low impedance circuit for driving low frequencies, the circuit will burn just like fuse burn. In this way, the low impedance circuit allows only mid and high frequencies.

Spur, Overtones lies in between fundamental frequency and its harmonics.

Note: The digital harmonics tools or digital harmonics plugins always create aliasing that lie in human hearing range which never sounds musical to the human ears.

2.3.2.2. *Filters*:

The purpose of using a filter is to cutoff unwanted sounds that are not pleasant to human ears.

It provides a frequency selection knob at which the frequencies used to cut off and allow the other frequencies to pass through.

It provides a slope selector knob to reduce an amount of sound pressure level per octave.

It provides a bandwidth selector knob (Q-factor) to create a resonating bump at cut-off frequency to emulate the sound of one of the audio signal processing units during mixing process.

e.g:- Elysia niveau Filter, bx_subfilter

Types of Filters:

High-pass Filter allows the high frequency sounds to pass through and rejects the low frequency sounds. It is also known as Low-cut Filter. It provides a frequency selection knob below which the frequencies used to cut off along with lower frequencies and above which it allows the frequencies along with high frequencies to pass through. For High-pass Filter, we use a longer slope (6dB/Octave at max).

Low-pass Filter allows the low frequency sounds to pass through and rejects the high frequency sounds. It is also known as High-cut Filter. It provides a frequency selection knob above which the frequencies used to cut off along with high frequencies and below which it allows the frequencies along with low frequencies to pass through. For Low-pass Filter, we use a shorter slope (96dB/Octave at max).

We can use a combination of High-pass Filter and Low-pass Filter to create a Band-pass Filter or a Band-reject Filter.

A Band-pass Filter allows a band of selected frequencies to pass through and rejects the cut-off frequencies.

A Band-reject Filter or Band-stop Filter cuts-off a band of selected frequencies to reject and allows the cut-off frequencies to pass through.

2.3.2.3. *Equalisers (EQs)*:

Use of most of the EQs introduce phase issues. So, it is better to avoid equalisers for audio signal processing.

Absolute Phase Issue - If an audio signal is out of phase by 180 degree to the other audio signal, the sum of these two signal provide zero output. It means, the signals are fully cancelled to each other and you won't hear any sound when those two signals are summed.

Relative Phase Issue - If an audio signal is delayed by a certain time period in milli seconds to the original signal, then the fundamental frequency of original signal and its over tones at low frequency ranges vanishes and the sum of these two signal provide a brighter sound. If two signals are in-phase (zero degree out of phase), then when you sum those two signals the loudness used to be doubled or increased. If Relative Phase issue arises, the delayed signal cancels the low frequency ranges of the original signal and sounds "brighter (more treble sound)" to our ears but won't sound "louder" than the original signal when you sum those two signals. In relative phase issue, a time delay of one waveform occurs with out fully phase cancellation to the other waveform (partial phase cancellation).

Reasons to use an EQ

1. To interlock EQs of 2 or more similar sounding instruments that play at the same time period (Kick and Bass, Lead Vocal and Backing Vocals, Acoustic Guitars... etc) for mono compatibility
2. To use Emphasis and De-emhasis Techniques
3. For Tonal Harmony - To glue two instruments or more than two instruments that must sound cohesive and use similar colour blend such as Blue - Green, Red - Orange, Yellow - Lime
4. For Tonal Contrast - To differentiate two instruments or more than two instruments by using opposite colour contrast such as Yellow - Blue, Red - Green, Yellow - Red, Green - White - Red

Types of Equalisers (EQs):

Symmetrical EQ - It boosts wide and cuts wide.

It is useful for additive EQ (Addition of loudness at a certain frequency bandwidth)

e.g.:- Symmetric Equalisers manufactured by SSL, API, NEVE, HARRISON

Asymmetrical EQ - It boosts wide and cuts narrow.

It is useful for subtractive EQ, also known as Surgical EQ (Addition of loudness at a certain frequency bandwidth)

e.g.:- Helios 69 (An Inductor Based EQ that uses Ceramic Core Inductor or Phenolic Core Inductor for high Q-Factor value in High Frequency Applications), British EQ (Cambridge EQ, Oxford EQ)

Note: Both Ceramic Core and Phenolic Core Inductors don't have any magnetic properties

Active EQ - Phase shifts at centre frequency, if you change any EQ curve. Phase cancellation may occur with other waveforms. e.g:- Parametric EQ (Modular type EQ such as SSL G Series and E Series)

Passive EQ - Phase won't change, if you change any EQ curve. e.g:- Linear Phase EQ (A Digital EQ), Pultec EQ are useful for tonal contrast and mastering but not useful for transient sounds

Linear Phase EQ - It never change the phase of the sound. It is useful for sustained sound but not useful for transient sound (less sustained sound, having less release of the sound's envelope) because of pre-roll of the transients that sounds un-natural.

Shelving EQ - Useful to create Baxandal Curve (Useful for Emphasis De-emphasis, Mix bus processing, e.g:- Dangerous BAX EQ), Gerzon Curve (e.g:- Pultec EQ)

Graphic EQ - It has 6dB or 12dB gain control at each Fixed Frequency, Useful for correcting feedback issues at master output during Live Sound Scenario. It is also used for interlocking microphones on stage with nearby monitor speakers kept for performers to avoid feedback issues. e.g:- API 560, SPL Free Ranger by Plugin Alliance

Minimum Phase EQ - It is useful to analyse frequency response of acoustics of the environment without any latency. Such EQs are widely used in Real-time Analysers (a Hardware Unit). It is not useful for Audio Pre-production process specially in multiple miking setup for sound recording.

Note:- A Capacitor is good at creating High Pass Filter which allow you to hear high frequencies by roll-off low frequencies. An Inductor is good at creating Low Pass Filter which allow you to hear low frequencies by roll-off high frequencies.

2.3.2.4. *Dynamic Processors:* *Compressors, Limiters, Expanders, Noise-gates, De-essers*

Dynamic processors are used to control distance parameter, dynamics using distance parameter and loudness.

Compressors:

A compressor is made up of transformer(s) with vacuum tube(s) or transistor(s).

Reasons to use a Compressor

1. To control Envelope of the waveform and Dynamic Range.
2. To strengthen the weaker audio signals and make it audible clearly. It is also used to add more density of reverb and echo sounds.
3. To calibrate the damping factor of the cheapest speakers used during Live Sound Reinforcement because cheapest speakers used to have very poor damping factor.
4. It is used for harmonics addition. It won't introduce any phase issues to the audio signal. It could be the best substitute of Active EQ.

Types of Compressors:

Variable MU (Tube) Compressor (Fairchild 660, 670, Klanghelm MJUC Jr., Telefunken U73, Manley Vari MU, Altec 436C, HCL Varies, EMI TG 12413, UA 175B)

1. Provides Slow Attack Time, Slow Release Time
2. Adds even harmonics (sounds smooth and transparent). It has more impedance value.
3. Ratio increases with gain reduction; it uses re-biased vacuum tube for gain reduction
4. Contains non-linear transfer curve
5. Its behaviour is based on RMS value of the input signal
6. Operating it with out a side chain filter will kill the bass, will not sound punchy ; not useful for bringing punchy sound
7. Sounds rounder, softer, smoother and adds depth, texture, definition
8. Fairchild Compressor contains 32 Transformers and 11 Tubes
9. Audio signal processing happens through these transformers and vacuum tubes

Note: Laminated Core Inductors are more common in Audio Transformers

10. Controls gain of a re-biased vacuum tube with no attack knob
11. Bias knob adjusts bass frequencies
12. Useful for fat and explosive sound such as Drums, Vocals, Bowed String ensemble, Brass ensemble, Woodwind ensemble... etc.

Optical (Tube) Compressor (LA 2A, LA 3A, Tube Tech CL1B)

1. Provides Slow Attack Time, Slow Release Time
2. Adds even harmonics (sounds smooth, transparent). It has more impedance value.

3. Its behaviour is based on RMS value of the input signal
4. Adds low frequency harmonics which cause standing waves
5. Use HPF in side chain while using in a mix
6. It contains a vacuum tube at the output section for gain stage
7. On Vocals and Bass use LA2A, On Electric Clean Guitar use LA3A

Field-effect Transistor based Compressor (FET 1176, API 2500)

1. Provides Fast Attack Time, Fast Release Time
2. Adds odd harmonics at mid and high frequencies, sounds edgy and coloured like square waves. It has less impedance value.
3. Can be used as line amplifiers
4. Most of them doesn't have a side chain filter; so not suitable for mix bus compression
5. Adds bite, punch, attitude to the sound
6. Useful on Vocals, Plucked String instruments

Note: The Field Effect Transistor controls the voltage where as a normal Transistor controls the current in the audio electronic circuit of the audio equipment.

VCA Compressor (DBX 160, Vertigo VSM3, Focusrite Red 3)

1. Provides Fast Attack Time, Fast Release Time
2. Adds odd harmonics at mid & high frequencies, sounds edgy like square waves and coloured too. It has less impedance value.
3. Its behaviour is based on PEAK value of the input signal
4. Used on mix bus & master bus to glue all the signals routed from the channels to sub groups(Auxes) & sub groups to the master
5. Adds aggression
6. Useful on Drum sub group, Percussion sub group

Note: When you use low ratio in a dbx 160 VCA Compressor, attack time used to be slow (more) and release time used to be fast (less). When you use high ratio in a dbx 160 VCA Compressor, attack time used to be fast (less) and release time used to be slow (more).

Digital Compressor (Waves C1)

1. Very transparent compressor
2. All parameters can be used according to the input signal of the sound source type (louder, softer, low, mid, high, transient, sustained, envelope characteristics...etc)

Single-band Compressor (De-esser)

1. Dynamics of a selected band of frequencies can be controlled separately where as dynamics of rest of the audible frequencies remain unchanged. A de-esser is used to control sibilance (a high frequency band whose centre frequency could be 6KHz, 9KHz or 12 KHz).But now-a-days we use it for any frequency band having issues such as controlling muddiness of the upper bass frequency band and lower mid frequency band or controlling presence of the vocal between 3KHz to 4KHz frequency range.

Multi-band Compressor (Harrison Console's Multi-band Compressor, Tokyo Dawn Lab's TDR Nova)

1. Dynamics of multiple band of frequencies can be controlled individually (which means a compressor is available for each band of frequencies).
2. It is popularly used in mastering process.

Limiter (Vladislav Goncharov's Limiter No 6, Audio Damage Inc's Rough Rider 3, Precision Limiter, Chandler Limited Zener Limiter, Sonnox Oxford Limiter, C-Suite C-Max Limiter)

1. Above the threshold level, it pull back the audio signal.
2. It won't allow the audio signal above the threshold level.
3. It can be used as a magnifying glass to monitor minute change in audio signal processing of each band of frequencies
4. It is popularly used in mastering process.
5. Most of the compressor has limiting features. e.g:- *Manley Vari Mu, Fairchild 670, 1176 collection, dbx 160, Neve 2254/E, 33609/C*

Expander

1. It pushes away the audio signals above and below the threshold level.
2. It is useful for compressing the loudness of a constant audible noise and masking it with enhanced audio signals. Because below the threshold level, the noise can be compressed and above the threshold level the audio signal can be enhanced.
3. At the output of an expander, the compressed noise is not audible as compared to enhanced audio signal.
4. Most of the channel strips such as Neve 88RS, SSL E series, API Vision Channel Strip, used to have noise gate and expander.

Noise Gate

1. Above the threshold level, it allows the audio signal but below the threshold level, it won't allow the audio signal.
2. The time taken to react a noise gate depends on attack time (time taken to open noise gate) and release time (time taken to close a noise gate).

Envelope Shaper

1. It shapes the envelope of the audio signal using attack, decay, sustain and release parameters.

2. Basically it is used to change the length of sustain of the sound.

2.3.2.5. *Echo and Reverb*

According to the Haas effect, so called Precedence effect, our brain is not able to differentiate less than 25 milli seconds of time delay between direct sound and reflected sound. Human brain assumes that the reflected sound is a tail part of direct sound which is not true. Such effect perceived by human brain is known as Reverb. But the human brain can easily differentiate more than 35 milli seconds of time delay between direct sound and reflected sound. In this case, each reflected sound can be a delayed reverb sound. So the effect of repetitive reverb sound for a limited time period perceived by human brain is called as Echo. Echo can be experienced at a huge outdoor areas such as hill stations where as reverb can be experienced at a small indoor areas such as bathrooms that contain tiles on the floor and walls.

The repetition of the direct raw sound doesn't exist in nature. But we can create such delay effect using a digital audio equipment, known as delay designer.

There are 2 types of reverb widely used. Spring reverb(e.g:- AKG BX20, Valhalla Shimmer) add shimmer from 15KHz onwards which is useful for transient sounds such as snare, strumming on acoustic guitar... etc. Plate reverb(e.g:- Pure Plate Reverb, Valhalla Plate) add a certain edge at upper mid frequencies from 2.5KHz to around 12KHz which is useful for sustained sounds such as lead vocal, electric guitar... etc. Plate reverb sounds darker and feels like mono, a point source where as spring reverb sounds brighter and feels like binaural stereo spread, a line source.

An echo effect can be created digitally by adding reverb to the repetitive delayed sound of the direct raw sound for a limited time period or adding repetitive delay for a limited time period to the reverb sound.

Steps to create Channel Strips, Digital Console, Digital Audio Workstation, Plugins:

1. Conceptualise and Design using one of Development Environment Frameworks such as Sigma Studio by Analog Devices, Audio Weaver by DSP Concepts, JUCE and many more
2. Develop a visually appealing, intuitive, interactive Graphic User Interface
3. Check for hardware and software integration, compatibility and performance optimisation which means minimum CPU usage and maximum efficiency
4. Ensure proper functioning and stability of your products
5. Join Creative Community fore more help, feedback and promotion of your designed products

Home Work:

Create a plugin using any one of the Graphic User Interfaces given below using following informations:

Purpose: Introducing a time saving simplified Audio Signal Routing and Mapping feature by integrating Sound Mixing Methods at Insert Section and redesigning Insert Section accordingly

1. INPUT SECTION:

KNOBS:
GAIN/TRIM = Preamp's Input Gain from - 20 dB to + 70 dB
PHASE = -180 degree to +180 degree

BUTTONS:
MIC/LINE/RTA = Mic input to Line input to Real-time Analyser switcher and vice-versa
RTA: Real-time Analyser for calibration purpose that detect and eliminate problems of the acoustically untreated space

+48 VOLT = Phantom power for Condenser Microphone's Input

NOISE CONTROL = Noise and Ambiance suppressor through Noise and Ambiance Signals' detection and elimination

HPF = High Pass Filter below 70 Hz, 80 Hz or 100 Hz

UNLINK/MS = A Multi Functional Button with Left Mono Signal Only + Right Mono Signal Only + Mid Centre Mono Signal Only + Sides Stereo Signal Only for separate Audio Signal Processing or Stereo Linked signal for equal Audio Signal Processing for both Left and Right Channels' Signals

PAD = -20 dB Gain Reduction

2. AUDIO SIGNAL PROCESSING SECTION:

KNOBS:

PAN = Positioning the sound to Left, Centre or Right of 3 Dimensional Space Environment on X axis

WIDTH = Width enhancement of a Stereophonic Sound on X axis, Width Knob will be inactive/bypassed for Monophonic Sound

FLAVOUR = A mix knob for a combination of Even Harmonics Addition and Odd Harmonics Addition

BAND PASS SHELVING = 12dB per octave Shelving cut of Low Frequencies below 250 Hz and 24 dB per octave Shelving cut of High Frequencies after 8KHz at BOTTOM, 12 dB per octave Shelving cut of Low Frequencies below 250 Hz at CENTRE, 12 dB per octave Shelving cut of Low Frequencies below 20 Hz at BOTTOM

DYNAMICS = Enhance weaker signals ranging from 2:1 ratio (near) to 10:1 ratio (far)

FX = A mix knob for a combination of Bright Reverb (Shimmery Spring Reverb with more Width, Low pass Shelving and 8 milli second pre-delay) and Dark Reverb (Chamber Plate Reverb with less Width, High pass Shelving and 200 ms pre-delay)

DISTANCE = It controls 3 Dimensional Parameters such as WIDTH KNOB, FLAVOUR, SHELVING TILT, DYNAMICS, FX except PAN knob

3. OUTPUT SECTION:

KNOBS:
DISTANCE = A single 3D Knob (that indicates near, mid, far from left to right) for Routing-Mapping VST to control signal processors' parameters (PAN KNOB, WIDTH KNOB, FLAVOUR, SHELVING TILT, DYNAMICS/BIAS, FX)
LINE OUT = Speaker Output Knob, this knob can also be routed to linear fader of the channel of user's DAW

BUTTONS:
DIRECT = Direct Button for Analog Audio Signal Monitoring during Sound Recording
MONO = To check phase issue of the stereophonic processed signal
DIM = - 20 dB Gain Reduction at the output for 2 way loudness (volume) Audio Signal Monitoring at the output
3D SPACE ANALYSER = An LCD that display the Sound Stage (3D Space Environment) where each channel's sound placement can be shown by default as a point source (one colour coded dot according to its frequency response) for monophonic sound and a line source (two similar colour coded dots connected with similar coloured line according to its frequency response) for stereophonic sound. The sound placement could be Left, Centre, Right for X Axis, Bottom, Mid, Top for Y Axis, Near, Mid, Far on Y Axis. Therefore the number of minimum sound placement possibilities could be 27. So we could have 27 number of coordinates at minimum for sound placements to be shown on the LCD Display that indicates preset of the Audio Signal Processors' parameter values (the values of PAN, WIDTH, FLAVOUR, SHELVING TILT, DYNAMICS/BIAS, FX).

ADDITIONAL BUTTONS:
PREV = Switching to previous audio channel, previous channel's command of the user's DAW will be assigned to this button
NEXT = Switching to next audio channel, next channel's command of the user's DAW will be assigned to this button

FCN/MIDI LEARN = A 3D Control Multifunctional Menu Button that contains 15 inserts assigned to
10 knobs (GAIN/TRIM, PHASE KNOB, PAN KNOB, WIDTH KNOB, FLAVOUR, SHELVING TILT, DYNAMICS/BIAS, FX),
2 Buttons (NOISE CTRL and RTA Buttons),
3 inserts can be used for multi-metering VSTs.
The rest 8 buttons (except PREV, NEXT, FCN, ANALYSER) can be assigned (mapped and routed) to their respective functions' ON/OFF switches of their respective channels
The FCN Button is also capable of adding, removing, enabling, disabling functions and inserts
ANALYSER = Display the Sound Stage (3D Space Environment) where each channel's sound placement can be shown by default. It is a multifunctional button that displays output multi metering if inserted at the inserts of 3D Button, also displays plugin parameters if opened

4.   Signal Mapping/Routing Method for each knob using 3D Button:-

Step 1:   Create a knob/button/slider by clicking on '+' button.
Step 2:   Rename the button/knob and its parameters' value according to its function. Right click to '+' button to assign single or multi-parameters to the knob/button
Step 3:   Long press FCN or right click on knob to enable MIDI LEARN functionality for signal mapping and routing
Step 4:   Move the knob (FX) at extreme left, then enable MIDI LEARN functionality by long press FCN button or right click on the knob to choose MIDI LEARN function
Step 5:   choose a 3rd party VST plugin (say, LEXICON 480L DIGITAL REVERB) as an insert of channel strip / auxiliary / master for knob assignment (say, the knob is named as FX)

Step 6:   Open the VST Plugin assigned (LEXICON 480L DIGITAL REVERB) and move all the knobs and faders of the VST Plugin to achieve desired sound (say, Shimmery Spring Reverb with Low pass Shelving and 8 milli second pre-delay to achieve BRIGHT REVERB sound)

Step 7:   Save the VST Parameter Values as a preset (snapshot) for extreme left position of the single knob assignment by pressing FCN/MIDI LEARN button once

Step 8:   Move the knob (FX) at extreme right, then enable MIDI LEARN functionality by long press FCN button or right click to choose MIDI LEARN function

Step 9:   Open the VST Plugin assigned (LEXICON 480L DIGITAL REVERB) and move all the knobs and faders of the VST Plugin to achieve desired sound (Chamber Plate Reverb with High pass Shelving and 48 milli second pre-delay to achieve DARK REVERB sound)

Step 10: Save the VST Parameter Values as a preset (snapshot) for extreme right position of the single knob assignment by pressing FCN/MIDI LEARN once or right click to choose Save Preset function

Step 11: Verify the smooth transition from left to right or right to left of the knob will effect the parameters of all knobs and faders of VST plugin

Step 12: Right click FCN/MIDI LEARN to save as custom preset of signal mapping and routing of all buttons and knobs

Repeat the same process for HP OUT/3D knob to control WIDTH KNOB, FLAVOUR, SHELVING TILT, DYNAMICS, FX

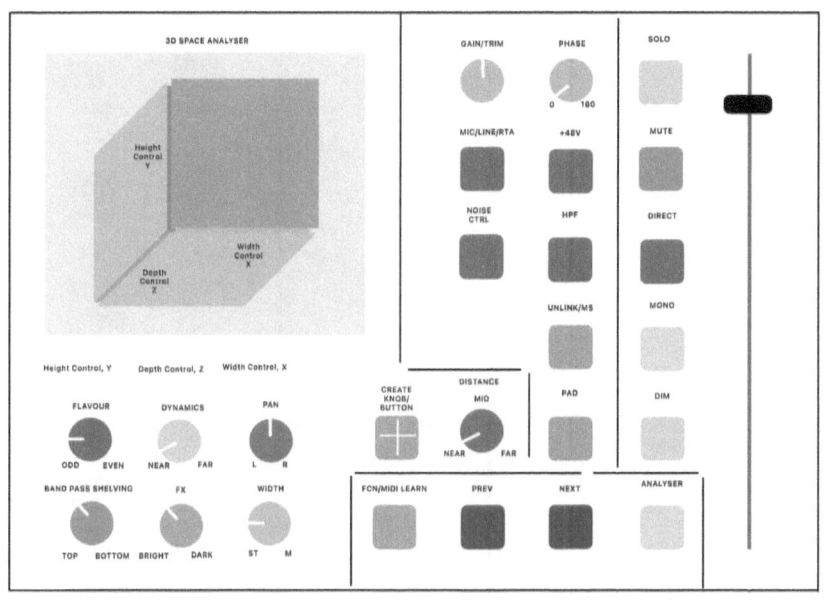

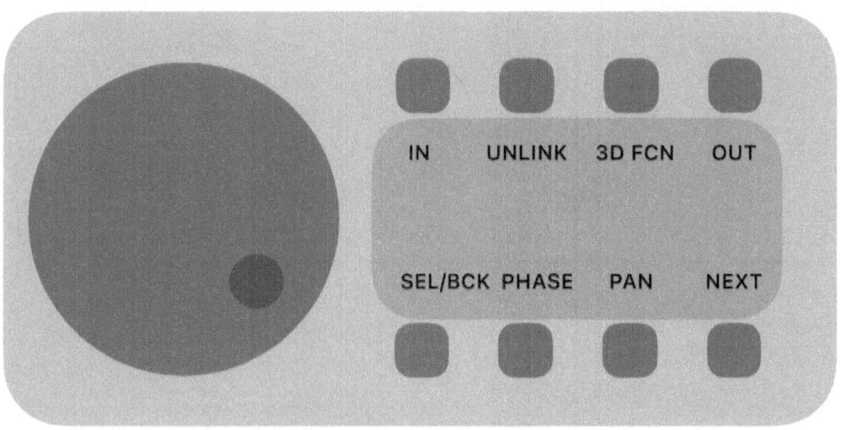

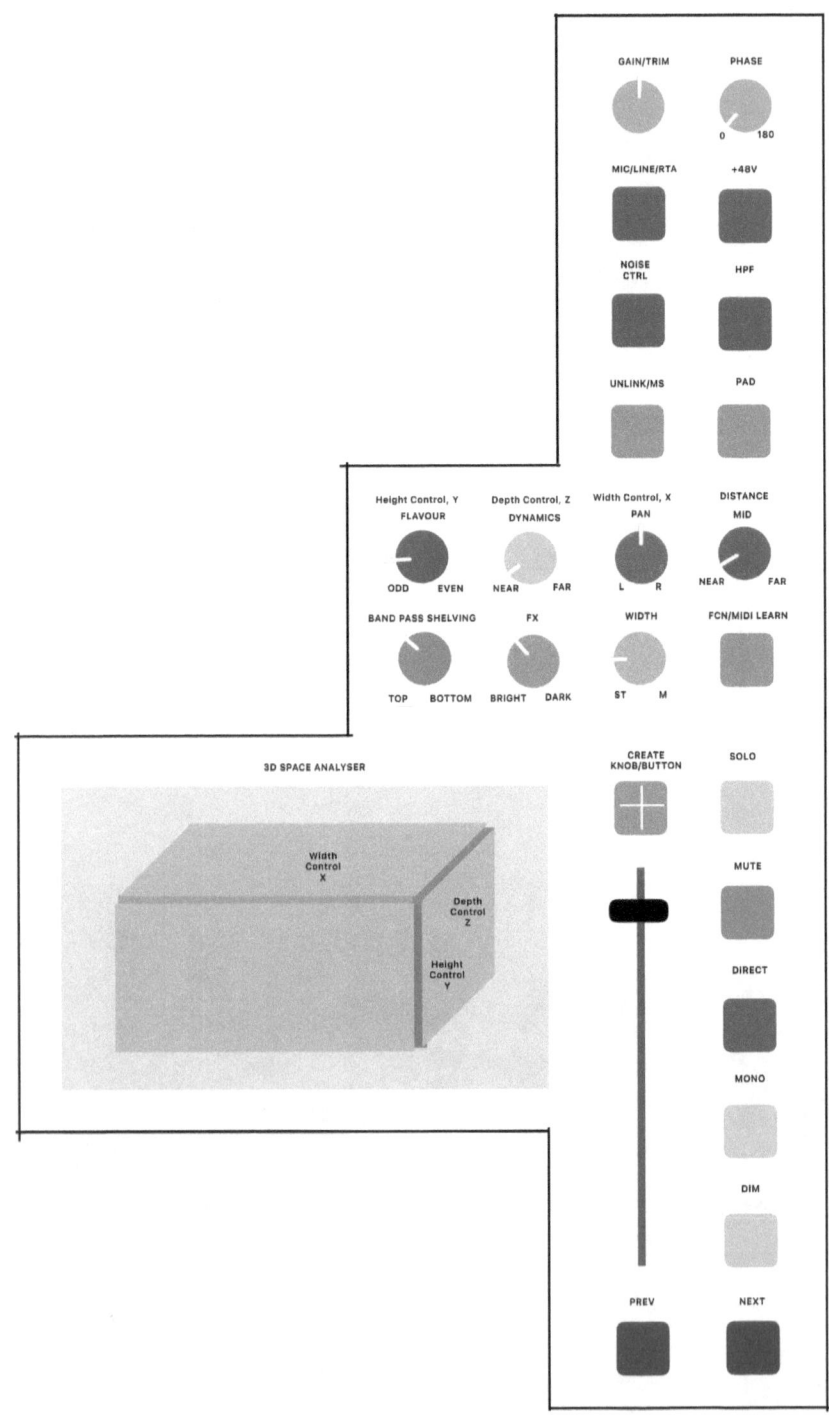

CRAFT YOUR SOUND

3D SPACE ANALYSER

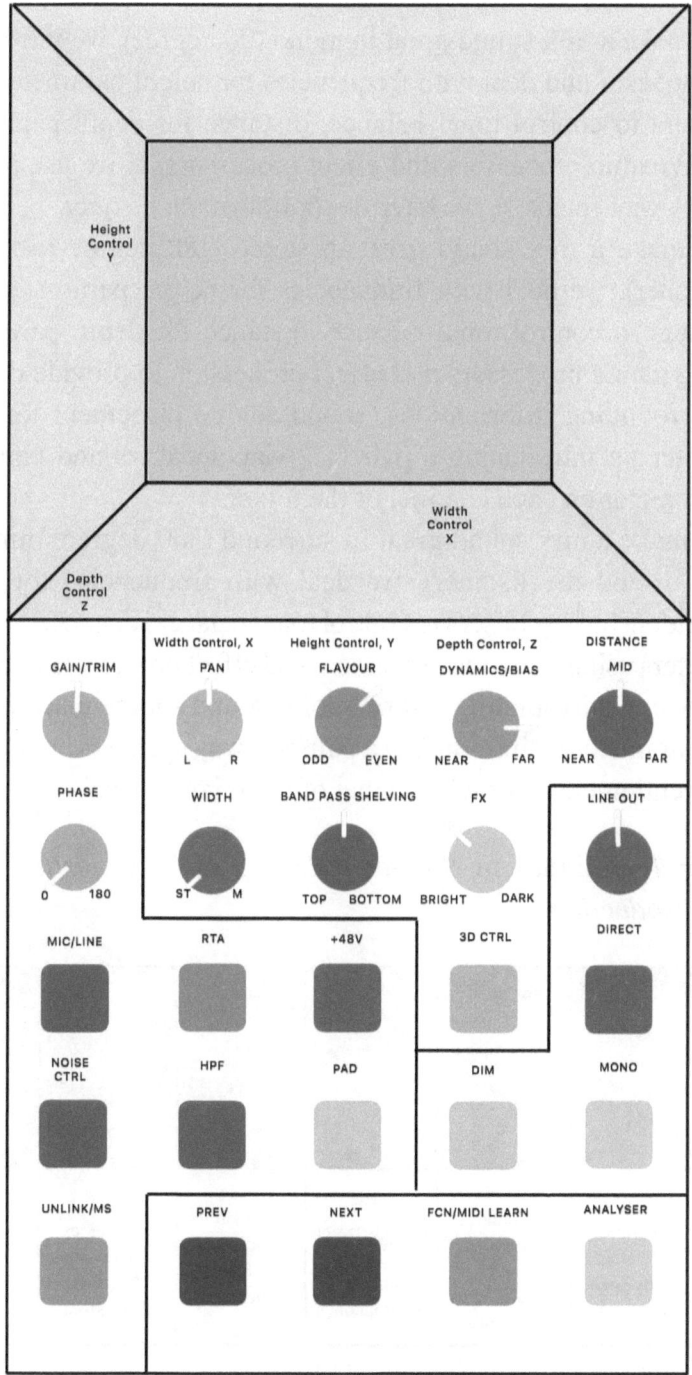

GIRISH PATRO

2.3.3. Introduction to Mixing Techniques:

To make a mix sound great in mono (90 degree), we introduce a 2 way speaker and deal with frequencies for height parameter using equalisers to control tonal balance, distance for depth parameters using dynamic processors and effect processors. If we use a single driver (1 way speaker), we have depth informations only.

To make a mix sound great in stereo (180 degree in-front of the listener), we deal with frequencies for height parameter using equalisers to control tonal balance, distance for depth parameters using dynamic processors and effect processors to provide distance and surrounding informations, sound source placement for width parameter by introducing a pair of 2-way speakers and panaroma potentiometer on each channel of the mixer.

To make a mix sound great in surround (360 degree immersive sound around the listener), we deal with frequencies for height parameter using equalisers to control tonal balance, distance for depth parameters using dynamic processors and effect processors to provide distance and surrounding informations, sound source placement for width parameter by introducing a pair of 2-way speakers at minimum and potentiometer on each channel of the mixer.

Mixing Techniques in Stereo: Role of Psycho-acoustics during Audio Production

Para meters of 3D Space Environment	Subjective Quantity (Measured by Ears)	Objective Quantity (Measured by Machines)	Tools and Techniques to capture a natural 3D Space Environment	Tools to be used to create a natural 3D Space Environment	Purpose to be Observed Aurally at Front Object Aux (Lead Instruments)	Purpose to be Observed Aurally at Rear Bed Aux (Backing Instruments)
Depth on Z-axis	Relative Volume (Loudnes) with Room Response	Front, Rear Sound Pressure Level according to Distance	3:1 Distance Ratio between a Sound Source and Microphones	1. Dynamics Processors 2. Effect Processors	Odd Harmonics Dynamics & Effect Processors	Even Harmonics Dynamics & Effect Processors

Para meters of 3D Space Environment	Subjective Quantity (Measured by Ears)	Objective Quantity (Measured by Machines)	Tools and Techniques to capture a natural 3D Space Environment	Tools to be used to create a natural 3D Space Environment	Purpose to be Observed Aurally at Front Object Aux (Lead Instruments)	Purpose to be Observed Aurally at Rear Bed Aux (Backing Instruments)
Height on Y-axis	Pitch	Frequency	Microphones' Selection	1. Filters 2. EQs	Odd Harmonics EQ & Filters	Even Harmonics EQ & Filters
Width on X-axis	Position or Location (Left or Right)	Front - Rear, Left - Right Loudness Difference for Sound Localisation	Mono, Stereo or Multiple Array Miking	1. Width Enhancer 2. Pan Knob 3. Binaural Processing Unit	More Width	Less Width

Audio Signal Processors:

Harmonics Choices by Manufacturers	Audio Signal Processors	Digital Products
American Companies use Transistor based Audio Products that produce Odd Harmonics	FET EQs	API 550, API 560
	FET Compressors	API 2500, Teletronix FET 1176, Neve 2254/E, Neve 33609/C
	Spring Reverbs	AKG BX 20, Valhalla Shimmer
German & British Companies use Vacuum Tube (Valve) based Audio Products that produce Even Harmonics	Tube EQs	Pultec EQP 1A, MEQ 5, REDD 17, 37-51, UA 610, Shatterglass Audio Code Redd Free
	VariMu Compressors	Fairchild 660, 670, UA 175B, Klanghelm MJUC Jr., Telefunken U73
	Optical Compressors	Manley Voxbox, Teletronix LA2A, LA3A, Tubetech CL1B MKII
	Plate Reverbs	Pure Plate Reverb, Valhalla Plate Reverb
	Chamber Reverbs	Capitol Chambers

Harmonics Choices by Manufacturers	Audio Signal Processors	Digital Products
American Companies (Odd Harmonics), German & British Companies (Even Harrmonics)	Console EQs (Tape based)	Odd - API 550, 560 Even - Neve 1073, 1084, Focusrite Red 2
	VCA Compressors and Channel Strips	Odd - SSL4000 E, SSL 4000 G, SSL 9000 J Even - dBx 160, Focusrite Red3, Vertigo VSM3, Harrison Console Multiband Compressor
	Non-linear Digital Reverbs	Lexicon 480L, Relab Development LX480
Natural & Transparent Sound Texture (Original)	Inductor EQs	Helios Type 69, Lindell Audio 69 by Plugin Alliance
	Digital EQs	Available in all DAWs
	Digital Compressors	Waves C1, L2, Sonnox Inflator, Logic Pro's Adaptive Limiter
	Digital Delays	Available in all DAWs, Valhalla Delay
	Stereo Width Widening Tools	EQ with Mid-Side Processing such as Shatterglass Audio Code Redd Free, Logic Pro's Linear Phase EQ

Therefore, Sound Mixing is a process to create a contrast between Even Harmonics (for Secondary Instruments) and Odd Harmonics (for Lead or Primary Instruments). It is also a process of placements of propagated sounds from sound sources in a three dimensional space.

Use of Audio Signal Processors:

For Master Buss, we use Harrison Console's Mastering EQ and Multi-band Compressor, Tokyo Dawn Labs TDR Kotelnikov Mastering Compressor, Ampex ATR-102, Oxide Tape Recorder, Verve Analog Machine, Rough Rider 3 Limiter, Venomode's Maximal 2, Vladislav Goncharov's Limiter No6, Plugin Alliance's bx_Masterdesk Classic are used for Audio Signal Processing in

Stereo where as Shatterglass Audio's Code Redd Free EQ, Fairchild 670 and Vladislav Goncharov's Molot compressor/limiter are used for Mid-Side Processing during Mastering. Here we also use Tokyo Dawn Lab's Prism for Loudness Monitoring.

For Width Enhancer we use Plugin Alliance's bx_Masterdesk Classic, Infected Mushroom's Wider.

For Mix Buss/Auxiliaries, we use Focusrite Red 2 EQ, Focusrite Red 3 VCA Compressor, Softtube's VCA Compressor, dbx 160 VCA Compressor, Precision Channelstrip, Neve 88RS, Elisa Alpha Compressor, Fairchild 670, Vladislav Goncharov's Molot compressor/limiter, Studer A800, Oxide Tape Recorder, Tokyo Dawn's TDR Nova Dynamic EQ and all kinds of effect processors(Tape Delay, Tube Delay, Echo Chambers, Reverb Chambers such as Dream Verb, Real Verb Pro, Capitol Chambers, Valhalla DSP collections, Softtube TSAR 1R, Plate Reverb such as Pure Plate Reverb, Spring Reverb such as AKG BX 20) are used for Audio Signal Processing in Stereo. For Male Vocal Buss, FET 1176 Rev A and LA2A Grey are useful. For Drum Buss, we use Pultec EQP1A, Pultec MEQ5, Neve 33609/C, 1176 Rev E, Fairchild 670, LA2A Silver, V76, Elysia Alpha Compressor, Century Channel Strip. For Electric Guitar Buss, we use FET 1176 AE.

For Channel Strips, we use SSL 4000 E, Neve 88RS, API Vision Channel Strip, Century Tube Channel Strip, Manley Voxbox, Townsend Lab's Sphere, Shatterglass Audio Lab's Code Red Free.

For Phase correction, we use Little Labs IBP.

For all kinds of vocals, we use C-Suite C-Vox for ambiance and noise control, Helios Type 69, Manley Voxbox, Fuse Audio's VPre72, RAW Distortion Unit, V76. For Male Vocals, Fairchild 660 is useful. For Female Vocals Pultec EQP1A, Galaxy Tape Echo are useful.

For Bass Guitar, we use FET 1176 Rev E, Century Tube Channel Strip, Fairchild 660, Manley Voxbox, Plugin Alliance's bx_subfilter, Pultec EQP1A, Pultec HL1C, V76, Softtube Bass Amp Room 8x10, LA2A.

For Synth Bass and Kick Drum, we use Plugin Alliance's bx_ subfilter.

For Snare we use Neve 2254/E, 1176 Rev E or API 2500 Compressor

For all kinds of Guitars, we use C-Suite C-Axe for ambiance and noise control, FET 1176LN, V76. For Accoustic Guitars, C-Suite C-Axe for ambiance and noise control, Manley Voxbox, Pultec EQP1A are useful. For all Electric Guitars, C-Suite C-Axe for ambiance and noise control, LA2A Grey, V76, Pultec EQP1A, Pultec HL1C, Century Tube Channel Strip, Brigade Chorus, RAW Distortion, Galaxy Tape Echo, Marshall Plexi Classic, Ampeg SVTVR Classic are useful.

For Brass and Bowed String Instruments, we use Ribbon Microphone emulations available in Townsend Lab's Sphere, Tube based Audio Signal Processors (Fairchild 660, Vladislav Goncharov's Molot, Klanghelm's MJUC Jr., Pultec EQ Collections, UA 610 Collections)

For Piano, we use C-Suite C-Axe for ambiance and noise control and LA2.

For Electric Keys and Synths, we use Century Tube Channel Strip, Brigade Chorus, Galaxy Tape Echo.

For Wurlitzer, Pultec EQP1A is useful.

Note:

We use Even Harmonics (Second Order Harmonics) based Audio Signal Processing for Lead instruments during Slower Tempo.

We use Even Harmonics (Second Order Harmonics) based Audio Signal Processing for Supporting Instruments during Faster Tempo.

We use Odd Harmonics (Third Order Harmonics) based Audio Signal Processing for Lead instruments during Faster Tempo.

We use Odd Harmonics (Third Order Harmonics) based Audio Signal Processing for Supporting Instruments during Slower Tempo.

Note: In most of the studios, the sound engineers record the performances on acoustical instruments using Neve, Harrison Consoles where as they mix using API and SSL Consoles.

In Industry Standard Mixing Methods, we often find 2 Tier Mix which means, the Lead Instruments' channel strips' audio signals used to send to Front Stereo Auxiliary and Supporting Instruments' channel strips' signals used to send to Rear Stereo Auxiliary through stereo busses. The Front and Rear Stereo Auxiliaries' audio signals used to send to Master Channel.

The Front Stereo Auxiliary used to have more Width, more Height (Wider Frequency Range), less Depth (2:1 or 4:1 Ratio, Fast Attack, Fast Release, Hard Knee control in Dynamic Processor), less amount of Wider Brighter Reverb with 12 millisecond Pre-delay. For a desired amount of Depth Control using a Dynamic Processor, we can adjust threshold level to satisfy the ratio.

The Rear Stereo Auxiliary used to have less Width, less Height (Narrower Frequency Range compared to Front Stereo Auxiliary), less Depth (4:1 or 7:1 Ratio, Slow Attack, Slow Release, Soft Knee control in Dynamic Processor), more amount of Narrower Darker Reverb with 24 millisecond Pre-delay.

The Front Stereo image can be divided into 3 regions named as Front Left, Front Right, Front Centre. So, instead of using a Front Stereo Auxiliary, we can use 3 Auxiliaries named as Front Left(FL), Front Right(FR), Front Centre (FC).

The Rear Stereo image can be divided into 2 regions named as Rear Left, Rear Right. So, instead of using a Rear Stereo Auxiliary, we can use 2 Auxiliaries named as Rear Left(RL), Rear Right(RR).

Here are the industry standard mix methods as follows:

2.3.3.1. *Stereo Mixing Techniques 1: Dynamics Based 3 tier mix (Useful for Faster Tempo Songs)*

1. Insert **VU meter** plugin at each channel and put 0dBVU setting or insert a gain tool at each channels' insert and put -18dBFS setting. Find important elements (specially at the chorus and bridge parts) in the mix and decide their placements (Front, Middle, Rear, Left, Right of your stage or listening environment)
2. **Gain Staging** - Bring the context using each instrument by putting **pink noise** audio signal plugin or audio file on a track

and set its level at -6dB.Increase the level of each track up to a noticeable level by masking a little bit of that pink noise.

3. **Use of Filters** - Check whether the unwanted sounds are filtered or not. Also check **Phase** issues (**Absolute Phase** issues and **Relative Phase** issues).Use the tool Little Labs IBP for Phase Correction if required. Check whether the SPL of regions/clips of each track is properly balanced or not. Verify all the audio editing processes before mixing.

4. Create Aux tracks - Create 5 aux tracks

   (i) **Front Stereo Aux** - Sending those channels' signals (transient signals) which you want to put at the front of your mix or performing stage.

Create an aux and name it as "Front".Put a bus as pre-fader at the send insert of channel strip and set the bus as the front stereo aux input. Use distortion, envelope shaping plugins to get right kind of transient sound according to the tempo at the channel strip if required and make use of mix knob for a proper blend of raw dry signals and processed wet signals of each signal processing unit.

While using harmonic distortion to an instrument, start with high frequency instruments and end with low frequency instruments.

At the aux put a Compressor with the following settings:

more (slow) attack time and less (fast) release time
ratio at 4:1 (for slow and medium tempo), upto 8:1 (for faster tempo)
put hard knee control and threshold level at zero dB

Process:

a) Set the threshold level in such a way that the compressor will start acting and doing gain reduction as per the ratio setting (e.g. 3 dB gain reduction at output as compared to input of a compressor during 4:1 ratio for faster tempo)

b) Decrease the bus send (mix knob) of each track upto infinity and slowly increase upto a point when you feel the over tightness of the audio signal loose a bit and stop increasing level at that point (which means 95% Dry signal mixed with 5% Wet signal).Do it for each track that sent to front aux

Also try series processing using two or more compressors with less ratio settings (e.g. 1.2:1 ratio or 1.5:1 ratio).If two compressors used in series having **2:1** and **4:1** ratios respectively, the the total ratio will be {(2x4): (1x1)} = **8:1**.

(ii) **Middle Stereo Aux** - Sending those channels' signals (medium sustained signals) which you want to put at the middle of your mix or performing stage

Create an aux and name it as "Middle".Put a bus as pre-fader at the send insert of channel strip and set the bus as the middle aux input. Use distortion, envelope shaping plugins and delay plugin (that delays those tracks routed to Middle Stereo Aux) to get right kind of sustain sound according to the tempo at the channel strip if required and make use of mix knob for a proper blend of raw dry signals and processed wet signals of each signal processing unit.

While using harmonic distortion to an instrument, start with high frequency instruments and end with low frequency instruments.

At the aux put a Compressor with the following settings:

medium (average) attack time and medium (average) release time
ratio at 3:1 (for slower and medium tempo) and upto 6:1 (for faster tempo)
put average knee control
threshold level at zero dB

Process:

a) Set the threshold level in such a way that the compressor will start acting and doing gain reduction as per the ratio setting (e.g. 2 dB gain reduction at output as compared to input of a compressor at 3:1 ratio for slower and medium tempo)

b) Decrease the bus send's SPL of each track upto infinity and then slowly increase upto a point when you feel the over tightness of the audio signal loose a bit and stop increasing SPL at that point (which means 90% Dry signal mixed with 10% Wet signal).Do it for each track that sent to front aux.

Also try series processing using two or more compressors with less ratio settings (e.g. 1.2:1 ratio, 1.5:1 ratio)

Use 8 milli second delay at Middle Stereo Aux.

(iii) **Rear Stereo Aux** - Sending those channels' signals (more sustained signals) which you want to put at the rear of your mix or your performing stage.

Create an aux and name it as "Rear".Put a bus as pre-fader at the send insert of channel strip and set the bus as the rear aux input. Use distortion, envelope shaping plugins and delay plugin (that delays those tracks routed to Rear Stereo Aux) to get right kind of sustain sound according to the tempo at the channel strip if required and make use of mix knob for a proper blend of raw dry signals and processed wet signals of each signal processing unit.

While using harmonic distortion to an instrument, start with high frequency instruments and end with low frequency instruments.

At the aux put a Compressor with the following settings:

less (fast) attack time and more (slow) release time
ratio at 2:1 (for slower and medium tempo) and upto 4:1 (for faster tempo)
put soft knee control

threshold level at zero dB

To keep secondary sustained supporting instruments at the rear background (say guitar arpeggiator, synth guitar arpeggiator) use the following setting in optical compressor -

less (fast) attack time and more (slow) release time
ratio at 1.1:1 (for slower and medium tempo) & upto 2:1 (for faster tempo)
put soft knee control
threshold level at minimum

Process:

a) Set the threshold level in such a way that the compressor will start acting and doing gain reduction as per the ratio setting (e.g. 1 dB gain reduction at output as compared to input of a compressor at 2:1 ratio for faster tempo)

b) Decrease the bus send's SPL of each track upto infinity and then slowly increase upto a point when you feel the over tightness of the audio signal loose a bit and stop increasing SPL at that point (which means 80% Dry signal mixed with 20% Wet signal).Do it for each track that sent to front aux.

Also try series processing using two or more compressors with less ratio settings (e.g. 1.2:1 ratio, 1.5:1 ratio)
Use 24 milli second delay at Rear Stereo Aux.

(iv) **Lead Mono Aux** - Sending those channels' signals (Lead instruments' signals) which you want to put at the centre of your mix or your performing stage.

Create an aux and name it as "Lead Mono".Put a bus as pre-fader at the send insert of channel strip and set the bus as the rear aux input. Use distortion, envelope shaping plugins and delay plugin (that delays those tracks routed to Rear Stereo Aux) to get right kind of sustain sound according to the tempo at the channel strip if required and make use of mix knob for a proper blend of raw dry signals and processed wet signals of each signal processing unit.

While using harmonic distortion to an instrument, start with high frequency instruments and end with low frequency instruments.

At the aux put a Compressor with the following settings:

medium (average) attack time and medium (medium) release time
ratio at 3:1 (for slower and medium tempo) and upto 6:1 (for faster tempo)
put soft knee control
threshold level at zero dB

Process:

a) Set the threshold level in such a way that the compressor will start acting and doing gain reduction as per the ratio setting (e.g. 2 dB gain reduction at output as compared to input of a compressor at 3:1 ratio for slower and medium tempo)

b) Decrease the bus send's SPL of each track upto infinity and then slowly increase upto a point when you feel the over tightness of the audio signal loose a bit and stop increasing SPL at that point (which means 95% Dry signal mixed with 5% Wet signal).Do it for each track that sent to lead mono aux.

Also try series processing using two or more compressors with less ratio settings (e.g. 1.2:1 ratio, 1.5:1 ratio).

5. Use 2 volume monitoring techniques (based on Fletcher-Munson Loudness Contour) - Use pad switch to monitor at louder level and softer level (minimum audible level)

6. Use **Subtractive EQ** in any channel strip and aux if required - Cut down the unwanted frequencies below fundamental frequency using HPF with Gerson Filter Curve using a digital EQ

Use subtractive EQ if required - Boost the pleasant frequencies using analog emulated EQ plugins. During EQ of an instrument (say acoustic guitar), we alway try to make it sound better but also need to focus on what changes you are noticing in other instruments (similar range of frequency instruments such as vocals, piano, classical guitar, uklele…etc).

Fundamental frequency of each instrument is dedicated to each octave in the frequency spectrum (Low frequency range - Kick and Bass, Mid frequency range - Vocals, Electric Guitar Lead, High frequency range - Shaker, Hi-hat, Ride, Cymbal).Use interlocking EQ of similar frequency range of musical instruments.

Fundamental frequency of each instrument is dedicated to each octave in the frequency spectrum (Low frequency range - Kick and Bass, Mid frequency range - Vocals, Electric Guitar Lead, High frequency range - Shaker, Hi-hat, Ride, Cymbal).Use interlocking EQ of similar frequency range of musical instruments.

7. Use separate additional aux tracks for **Effect Processing** if necessary.

(i) For lead vocal, create three auxiliaries - left, centre, right. For left & right auxes use a Bright Reverb (spring reverb) with more HF using additive EQ.For centre aux use a Dark Reverb (plate reverb) with more MF using subtractive EQ. At each vocal aux, we can use 3 dynamic processors in the inserts such as Low Level Limiter (Waves L1, Sonnox Inflator, Logic Pro's Adaptive Limiter), SSL 4000E or LA2A, Blue Striped FET 1176 Rev A. At insert of a stereo track and stereo aux, use Audio Signal Processors from Multiple Mono (or Stereo with Link icon off) to process Left channel and Right channel separately. Flip the phase polarity of one of the stereo channel (Right Channel). If you are using Delay plugin from Multiple Mono (or Stereo with Link icon off), then set both Mono Delays to Project's Tempo (Reference Delay = 1 Minute/Tempo = 60000ms/

Tempo). Offset Left channel by delaying 5 to 25 ms below the project's tempo and offset Right channel by advancing 5 to 25 ms above the project's tempo for a Wider Delay experience. Also experiment with Multiple Mono Reverb and follow the same process by offsetting different pre-delays for both Left and Right Channels. Use Shelving Curve instead of filters on stereo auxes and stereo channels to maintain a better phase relationship.

(ii) Kick should sound pointed; if not, then

a) increase its fundamental frequency by increasing the bell curve from lower bandwidth to larger bandwidth (Q - factor) at its fundamental frequency while listening to the context (overall audio signals) - May be average Q factor at 60 Hz.

b) use a 60Hz sine wave generator on a new track and do the side-chaining (ducking) with kick using noise gate

If the combination of kick and bass gives louder LF range at master out, then use subtractive EQ with a narrow band at kick track to decrease the resonating frequency (not the fundamental frequency)

(iii) For snare, use a Dark Delay (delay with plate reverb).If you are not getting any fundamental frequency of snare then use a 200Hz or 400Hz sine wave generator on a new track and do the side chaining (ducking) with kick using noise gate

(iv) Bass Widening of a Mono Bass track for a slower tempo songs:

Send the Mono Bass track's audio signal to a stereo aux through a stereo bus. At the stereo bass aux, cutoff below 400 Hz using High Pass Filter at 1st insert. Add Saturation at 2nd insert and do audio signal processing as per required. At 3rd insert we can add a stereo reverb or multiple mono reverb and do audio signal processing as per required. Then we can mix the right proportion of mix of dry signal (original raw bass audio signal from the Mono Bass Channel) and wet signal (processed bass audio signal from the Stereo Bass Aux).

8. Use one of the **LCR Panning** of each channel (either hard to left, hard to right or centre)
9. **Monitor** the Mix using filters

   (i) Cut low frequencies upto 1KHz using HPF. Mid and High frequencies should sound crystal clear
   (ii) Cut high frequencies upto 500Hz using LPF.Kick and Bass instruments should sound separated, tight and punchy
   (iii) Use BPF by cutting low frequencies upto 1KHz using HPF and cutting high frequencies upto 4KHz using LPF.The mid frequency instruments such as lead vocal, electric guitar, synthesisers...etc should sound separated, crystal clear and prominent.

Note: For placing the drum elements, use overhead tracks as reference to pan individual elements

Before putting any signal processor on any channel and aux, do signal processing on master channel first as follows:

a) An VCA compressor (SSL 4000 G-Series, dBX 160, Focusrite Red 3, Softtube's VCA Compressor, Precission Channel Strip, Tokyo Dawn Lab's TDR Kotelnikov or Shadow Hills Mastering Compressor) to pump and breathe the song -

   At first reset the parameters. Fix an average ratio and auto release. Then set attack time, set release time as per tempo of the song, setup threshold level, setup ratio.

   To glue the tracks - Slow Attack, Fast Release, 3 dB gain reduction at output compared to its input (4:1 ratio)
b) A Passive EQ (Pultec EQP1A) or Symmetrical EQ (VEQ/ Neve 1073, Neve 1084, Harrison 32C)

   Never use a Linear Phase EQ on transient sounds because of pre-ringing before the fundamental frequency hits

c) Kick can de-ess the Bass Guitar at 60 Hz and dry lead vocal can de-ess the wet lead vocal at a certain frequency range (mid and highs)

d) A compressor can be used at the end of the signal chain in a Wet Lead Vocal channel for side chain with the Dry Lead Vocal

Use FET based compressor (FET 1176 Rev E, Neve 2254/E) on snare

For vocals, use an optical compressor (LA2A), a harmonic distortion in series processing and a reverb in parallel processing using time, size, damping, early reflection, pre-delay, room, dry/wet mix parameters. Engage EQ or bypass Filters of backing vocals and other lead instruments during Bridge and Chorus sections of the song through Automation. At Master channel or during Mastering, increase 0.5 dB of Chorus and Bridge sections of Side channels using Mid-Side processing through Automation.

To achieve a wider delay in any stereo tracks, use your preferred multiple mono delay or unlink the stereo delay to process left and right signals separately as follows:

Set both left and right delays to project tempo

Off set left channel's signal by delaying 7 to 20 ms below the project tempo

Offset right channel's signal by advancing 7 to 20 ms above the project tempo.

Note: For 2 - Tier Mix, front aux and back aux are used and middle aux never used.

2.3.3.2. Stereo Mixing Techniques 2: Dynamics Based (Useful for Faster Tempo Songs)

1. Insert **VU meter** plugin at each channel and put 0dBVU setting or insert a gain tool at each channels' insert and put -18dBFS setting
2. **Gain Staging** - Put pink noise plugin at Master Channel and set its level at -6dB.Increase the level of each track to do masking a little bit of the pink noise
3. Create Aux Tracks - Create 4 aux tracks

    (i)   **Crossover Stereo Aux** - Send those channels' signals (louder sustained signals) which you want to send to this post fader aux. Aux return need to be manipulated.

    (ii) **Drum Squash Stereo Aux** (Newyork Style Parallel Compression) - Send those channels' signals (louder transient signals) which you want to send to this post fader aux. Aux return need to be manipulated.

    (iii) **Lead Mono Aux** - Send those channels' signals (Lead instruments' signals) which you want to send to this post fader aux. Aux return need to be manipulated. Use Convolution Reverb.

    (iv) **LF Mono Aux** - Send those channels' signals (Bass instruments' signals) which you want to send to this post fader aux. Aux return need to be manipulated. Interlocking of Bass Guitar EQ with Kick EQ is needed.

4. Use **Subtractive EQ** in any channel strip and aux if required - Cut down the unwanted frequencies below fundamental frequency using HPF with Gerson Filter Curve using a digital EQ. Use Shelving Curve instead of filters on drums and percussions to avoid damage of in-phase relationship.

    Use subtractive EQ if required - Boost the pleasant frequencies using analog emulated EQ plugins. During EQ of an instrument (say acoustic guitar), we alway try to make it sound better but also need to focus on what changes you are noticing in other instruments (similar range of frequency instruments such as vocals, piano, classical guitar, uklele…etc).

Fundamental frequency of each instrument is dedicated to each octave in the frequency spectrum (Low frequency range - Kick and Bass, Mid frequency range - Vocals, Electric Guitar Lead, High frequency range - Shaker, Hi-hat, Ride, Cymbal).Use interlocking EQ of similar frequency range of musical instruments.

5. Use separate additional aux tracks for effect processing

(i) For lead vocal, create three auxiliaries - left, centre, right. For left and right auxiliaries use a Bright Reverb (spring reverb) with more HF using additive EQ.For centre aux use a Dark Reverb (plate reverb) with more MF using subtractive EQ.

(ii) Kick should sound pointed; if not, then

a) increase its fundamental frequency by increasing the bell curve from lower bandwidth to larger bandwidth (Q - factor) at its fundamental frequency while listening to the context (overall audio signals) - May be average Q factor at 60 KHz.

b) use a 60Hz sine wave generator on a new track & do the side chaining (ducking) with kick using noise gate

If the combination of kick and bass gives louder LF range at master out, then use subtractive EQ with a narrow band at kick track to decrease the resonating frequency (not fundamental frequency)

(iii) For snare, use a dark delay (delay with plate reverb).If you are not getting any fundamental frequency of snare then use a 200Hz or 400Hz sine wave generator on a new track & do the sjidechaining (ducking) with kick using noise gate

6. Use one of the **LCR Panning** of each channel (either hard to left, hard to right or centre)
7. **Monitor** the Mix using filters -

(i)   Cut low frequencies upto 1KHz using HPF.Mid & High frequencies should sound crystal clear
(ii) Cut high frequencies upto 500Hz using LPF.Kick and Bass instruments should sound separated, tight and punchy
(iii) Use BPF by cutting low frequencies upto 1KHz using HPF and cutting high frequencies upto 4KHz using LPF.The mid frequency instruments such as lead vocal, electric guitar, synthesisers...etc should sound separated, crystal clear & prominent.

2.3.3.3. *Stereo Mixing Techniques 3: Time Based (Useful for Slower Tempo Songs)*

1. Insert **VU meter** plugin at each channel and put 0dBVU setting or insert a gain tool at each channels' insert and put -18dBFS setting
2. **Gain Staging** - Put pink noise plugin at Master Channel and set its level at -6dB.Increase the level of each track to do masking a little bit of the pink noise
3. Create Aux Tracks - Create 3 aux tracks

(i) **Stereo Front Delay Aux** - pre fader, 80ms delay, send its output to reverb aux, bus send level to minimum (minus infinity), use more stereo width (180 degree binaural or apply stereo widening plugin at insert of front delay plugin or hard pan to left & right)
(ii) **Stereo Back Delay Aux** - pre fader, 40ms delay, send its output to reverb aux, bus send level to minimum (minus infinity), use less stereo width (45 degree binaural or apply stereo widening plugin at insert of front delay plugin or 25% pan to left & 25% pan to right)

(iii) **Mono Reverb Aux** - post fader, use average stereo width (90 degree binaural or apply stereo widening plugin at insert of front delay plugin or 50% pan to left & 50% pan to right) for pointed narrow reverb

4. Insert a Compressor at the master track with the following settings:

   medium (average) attack time & medium (medium) release time
   ratio at 4:1 (for slower and medium tempo) & upto 6:1 (for faster tempo)
   put average knee control
   threshold level at zero dB

Process:

   a) Set the threshold level in such a way that the compressor will start acting & doing gain reduction as per the ratio setting (e.g. 3 dB gain reduction for slower & medium tempo)
   b) Set the mix knob for proper blend of dry signal and compressed signal

5. Use Subtractive EQ in any channel strip and aux if required - Cut down the unwanted frequencies below fundamental frequency using HPF with Gerson Filter Curve using a digital EQ. Use Shelving Curve instead of filters on drums and percussions to avoid damage of in-phase relationship.

   Use subtractive EQ if required - Boost the pleasant frequencies using analog emulated EQ plugins. During EQ of an instrument (say acoustic guitar), focus on what changes you are noticing in other instruments (similar range of frequency instruments such as vocals, piano, classical guitar, uklele...etc)
   Fundamental frequency of each instrument is dedicated to each octave in the frequency spectrum (Low frequency range - Kick &

Bass, Mid frequency range - Vocals, Electric Guitar Lead, High frequency range - Shaker, Hi-hat, Ride, Cymbal).Use interlocking EQ to the sub groups

6. Use separate additional aux tracks for **Effect Processing**

    (i)   For lead vocal, create three auxiliaries - left, centre, right. For left and right auxes use a bright reverb (spring reverb) with more HF using additive EQ.For centre aux use a dark reverb (plate reverb) with more MF using subtractive EQ.
    (ii) Kick should sound pointed; if not, then

        a) increase its fundamental frequency by increasing the bell curve from lower bandwidth to larger bandwidth (Q - factor) at its fundamental frequency while listening to the context (overall audio signals) - May be average Q factor at 60 KHz.
        b) use a 60Hz sine wave generator on a new track & do the side chaining (ducking) with kick using noise gate

If the combination of kick and bass gives louder LF range at master out, then use subtractive EQ with a narrow band at kick track to decrease the resonating frequency (not fundamental frequency)

    (iii) For snare, use a dark delay (delay with plate reverb).If you are not getting any fundamental frequency of snare then use a 200Hz or 400Hz sine wave generator on a new track and do the side chaining (ducking) with kick using noise gate

7. Use one of the **LCR Panning** of each channel (either hard to left, hard to right or centre)
8. **Monitor** the Mix using filters -

    (i)   Cut low frequencies upto 1KHz using HPF.Mid and High frequencies should sound crystal clear

(ii) Cut high frequencies upto 500Hz using LPF.Kick and Bass instruments should sound separated, tight and punchy

(iii) Use BPF by cutting low frequencies upto 1KHz using HPF and cutting high frequencies upto 4KHz using LPF.The mid frequency instruments such as lead vocal, electric guitar, synthesisers...etc should sound separated, crystal clear and prominent.

To achieve a wider delay in any stereo tracks, use your preferred multiple mono delay or unlink the stereo delay to process left and right signals separately as follows:

Set both left and right delays to project tempo

Off set left channel's signal by delaying 7 to 20 ms below the project tempo

Offset right channel's signal by advancing 7 to 20 ms above the project tempo.

2.3.3.4. *Stereo Mixing Techniques 4: Signal Processing for individual instrument (Useful for Medium Tempo Songs)*

1. Lead Vocal: **Series Processing**

   (i) Use of **Filters** - Cut down absence of frequencies and unwanted/unpleasant frequencies

   (ii) Use of **Distortion** - To provide an attitude to the vocal and bring the pleasant harmonics which are not present in the original signal, put a distortion plugin in series.

While using harmonic distortion to an instrument, start with high frequency instruments and end with low frequency instruments.

   (iii) Use of **EQ** - During EQ of an instrument (say acoustic guitar), we alway try to make it sound better but also need to focus on what changes you are noticing in other instruments (similar range of frequency instruments such as vocals, piano, classical guitar, uklele...etc).

Fundamental frequency of each instrument is dedicated to each octave in the frequency spectrum (Low frequency range - Kick and Bass, Mid frequency range - Vocals, Electric Guitar Lead, High frequency range - Shaker, Hi-hat, Ride, Cymbal).Use interlocking EQ of similar frequency range of musical instruments.

Subtractive EQ - If the vocal sounds nasal or honkey, then cut the levels at 250Hz & 500Hz using digital EQ. Use Shelving Curve instead of filters on drums and percussions to avoid damage of in-phase relationship.

Additive EQ - Use analog emulated EQ if required

(iv) Use of **Compressor** - (Series processing of two compressors)

    a) To control consonant sounds (transients), put an FET compressor (1176AE) with following settings:

        less (fast) attack time and less (fast) release time
        high ratio (4:1)
        put hard knee control
        threshold level below the level of consonants (transients) which contains peaks & also dynamic in nature

    b) To keep vocal at same level, put an **Optical Compressor** (LA2A) in series at the vocal channel with the following settings

        medium (moderate) attack time and less (fast) release time
        less ratio (1.2:1)
        put hard knee control
        threshold level at the level of RMS value of vowel sound (sustain)

(v) Use of Depth - Do parallel processing using aux sends as follows:

On the vocal delay aux, put a delay plugin with pre delay of 1/16th note {(1/16) x (60000/Tempo)} milli second.

On the vocal reverb aux put a reverb plugin. To thicken up the vocal lead, duplicate the lead vocal track & apply a delay unit with 1/8th or 1/16th note delay at the insert of the duplicated track and in series, apply LPF with average slope (12 dB per octave) to cut below 600Hz for not to notice the delay effect by human brain

2. Bass: **Series Processing**

(i) Use of **Filters** - Cut down absence of frequencies and unwanted/unpleasant frequencies

(ii) Use of **Distortion** - To provide an attitude to the bass & bring the pleasant harmonics which are not present in the original signal, put a distortion plugin in series.

While using harmonic distortion to an instrument, start with high frequency instruments and end with low frequency instruments.

(iii) Use of **EQ** - During EQ of an instrument (say acoustic guitar), we always try to make it sound better but also need to focus on what changes you are noticing in other instruments (similar range of frequency instruments such as vocals, piano, classical guitar, uklele…etc).

Fundamental frequency of each instrument is dedicated to each octave in the frequency spectrum (Low frequency range - Kick and Bass, Mid frequency range - Vocals, Electric Guitar Lead, High frequency range - Shaker, Hi-hat, Ride, Cymbal).Use interlocking EQ of similar frequency range of musical instruments.

Additive EQ - Use analog emulated EQ if required

(iv) Follow the process to use **VCA Compressor** as described below.

   a) To control the transient sound, put a compressor with following settings

   less (fast) attack time and less (fast) release time
   high ratio (4:1)
   put hard knee control
   threshold level below the level of transients which contains peaks & louder sound which causes more dynamic range

   b) To keep sustain at same level, put an **Optical Compressor** or **VariMu Compressor** in series at the bass track with the following settings

   more (slow) attack time (half of kick attack time) & more (slow) release time.e.g. If Bass Attack Time is $1/4^{th}$ note (say 250 ms), then Kick Attack Time is $1/8^{th}$ note (say 500 ms)
   more ratio (maximum 6dB gain reduction, 7:1)
   put soft knee control
   threshold level at the level of RMS value of sustain sound

3. Kick: **Series Processing**

   (i) Use of **Filters** - Cut down absence of frequencies and unwanted/unpleasant frequencies
   (ii) Use of **Distortion** - To provide an attitude to the kick & bring the pleasant harmonics which are not present in the original signal, put a distortion plugin in series.

While using harmonic distortion to an instrument, start with high frequency instruments & end with low frequency instruments.

(iii) Use of **EQ** - During EQ of an instrument (say acoustic guitar), focus on what changes you are noticing in other instruments (similar range of frequency instruments such as vocals, piano, classical guitar, uklele...etc)

Subtractive EQ - Cut down the level below 55Hz & 900Hz with average slope (24 dB per octave) using digital EQ. Use Shelving Curve instead of filters on drums and percussions to avoid damage of in-phase relationship.

Fundamental frequency of each instrument is dedicated to each octave in the frequency spectrum (Low frequency range - Kick & Bass, Mid frequency range - Vocals, Electric Guitar Lead, High frequency range - Shaker, Hi-hat, Ride, Cymbal).Use interlocking EQ to the sub groups

Additive EQ - Use analog emulated EQ if required

(iv) Use of **FET Compressor** (Neve 2254/E)

a) To control the transient sound, put an FET Compressor (Neve 2254/E) with following settings

less (fast) attack time and less (fast) release time
high ratio (4:1)
put hard knee control
threshold level below the level of transients which contains peaks & louder sound which causes more dynamic range

b) To keep sustain at same level, put an **Optical Compressor** (LA2A Silver) or **VariMu Compressor** (Fairchild 660, Klanghelm MJUC Jr., Vladislav Goncharov's Molot,

Telefunken U73, UA 175B) in series at the bass track with the following settings

more (slow) attack time (half of kick attack time) and more (slow) release time.e.g:- If Bass Attack Time is $1/4^{th}$ note (say 250 ms), then Kick Attack Time is $1/8^{th}$ note (say 500 ms)
more ratio (maximum 6dB gain reduction, 7:1)
put soft knee control
threshold level at the level of RMS value of sustain sound

4. Snare: **Series Processing**

(i) Use of **Filters** - Cut down absence of frequencies and unwanted/unpleasant frequencies
(ii) Use of **Distortion** - To provide an attitude to the snare & bring the pleasant harmonics which are not present in the original signal, put a distortion plugin in series. While using harmonic distortion to an instrument, start with high frequency instruments & end with low frequency instruments.
(iii) Use of **EQ** - During EQ of an instrument (say acoustic guitar), focus on what changes you are noticing in other instruments (similar range of frequency instruments such as vocals, piano, classical guitar, uklele…etc)

Subtractive EQ - Cut down the level below 200Hz & 6KHz with average slope (24 dB per octave) using digital EQ
Fundamental frequency of each instrument is dedicated to each octave in the frequency spectrum (Low frequency range - Kick & Bass, Mid frequency range - Vocals, Electric Guitar Lead, High frequency range - Shaker, Hi-hat, Ride, Cymbal).Use interlocking EQ to the sub groups
Additive EQ - Use analog emulated EQ if required

(iv) Follow the process of using **VCA Compressor** as described below.

    a) To control the transient sound, put an VCA Compressor (Focusrite Red 3, Softtube's VCA Compressor, dbx 160) with following settings

       less (fast) attack time and less (fast) release time
       high ratio (4:1)
       put hard knee control
       threshold level below the level of transients which contains peaks & louder sound which causes more dynamic range

    b) To keep sustain at same level, put an **FET Compressor** in series at the snare track with the following settings

       more (slow) attack time (half of kick attack time) & more (slow) release time.e.g. If Bass Attack Time is $1/4^{th}$ note (say 250 ms), then Snare Attack Time is $1/8^{th}$ note (say 500 ms)
       more ratio (maximum 6dB gain reduction, 7:1)
       put soft knee control
       threshold level at the level of RMS value of sustain sound

(v) Use of **Depth** - Do parallel processing using aux sends as follows:

    On the snare mono aux (Centre), put a delay plugin with pre delay of $1/8^{th}$ note $\{(1/8) \times (60000/\text{Tempo})\}$ milli second. Send its output to the reverb unit.

5. To keep secondary sustained supporting instruments at the rear background (say guitar arpeggiator, synth guitar arpeggiator) use the following setting in **Optical Compressor**

less (fast) attack time and more (slow) release time
less ratio (such as 1.1:1 for slower and medium tempo and 2:1 for faster tempo)
put soft knee control
threshold level at minimum

6. Mix analogy through colours -

(i) **Tonal Contrast** - Use on sub group auxiliaries

To differentiate two instruments or more than two instruments, use opposite colour contrast such as Yellow - Blue, Red - Green, Yellow - Red, Green - White - Red

e.g.:- Green -> Rear (HF) -> Importance of HF on dholak -> Less SPL using less attack time on a compressor
Red -> Middle (MF) -> Importance of MF on vocal -> Medium SPL using moderate attack time on a compressor
White -> Front (LF) -> Importance of LF on tabla -> More SPL using more attack time on a compressor

(ii) **Tonal Harmony** - Use on channel strips

To glue two instruments or more than two instruments, use similar colour contrast such as Blue - Green, Red - Orange, Yellow - Lime

7. Use one of the **LCR Panning** of each channel (either hard to left, hard to right or centre)
8. **Monitor** the Mix using filters -

(i) Cut low frequencies upto 1KHz using HPF.Mid and High frequencies should sound crystal clear
(ii) Cut high frequencies upto 500Hz using LPF.Kick and Bass instruments should sound separated, tight and punchy

(iii) Use BPF by cutting low frequencies upto 1KHz using HPF and cutting high frequencies upto 4KHz using LPF.The mid frequency instruments such as lead vocal, electric guitar, synthesisers...etc should sound separated, crystal clear and prominent.

2.3.3.5. *Stereo Mixing Techniques 5: Dynamics Based (useful for Faster Tempo Songs)*

1. Insert a Signal Generator plugin at a mono channel and put 0 dBVU setting (calibrated as -18 dBFS) that generate 1KHz Sine wave frequency tone.
2. Send the 1KHz signal from that mono channel to 5 stereo auxiliaries through 5 buses in parallel processing (for the sake of tone generation, fatness, attitude, urgency and transparency of sound; these are the nature of different types of compressors which sound urgent, lazy, dark, sloppy, non-coloured)
3. Name the auxiliaries as Vari MU, Optical, VCA, FET, Digital and as the name suggests put such different types of Compressors in each auxiliaries
4. All the bus sends must be at zero dB from the mono channel to the auxiliaries. You can mute the master channel if the 1 KHz Sine wave irritate to your ears but always keep an eye on VU meter (should be calibrated 0 dBVU as -18dBFS)
5. Calibrate the compressors at the insert of the respective auxes using 1KHz pure tone (sine wave) signal generator whose SPL is -18dBFS.

Process:

Setup the parameters according to the nature of each compressor so that 1 dB gain reduction will happen at each type of compressor unit using 2:1 ratio (VCA and FET based compressors used to have fast attack time and fast release time, VariMu and Optical type compressors used to have slow attack time and slow release time, Digital based compressor's parameters can be set according to the nature of input signal to the compressor - Low Frequency means more attack time, High Frequency means less attack time, Less Sustain means less release time, More Sustain means more release time)

6. Recheck the gain stage (output gain of the compressor should be the same as input gain to the compressor; if not then add 1dB makeup gain to compensate the loss)

7. If possible, check with other frequencies and redo the calibration processes for each frequency (fundamental frequencies of all musical instruments such as 60Hz, 90 Hz, 120 Hz, 200 Hz, 240 Hz, 400 Hz, 500Hz, 800Hz, 900 Hz, 1KHz, 2KHz, 3KHz, 4KHz, 6KHz, 8KHz, 9KHz, 10KHz, 12KHz, 14KHz, 15KHz using the Sine Wave Signal Generator).

8. Now disable that signal generator that has inserted in a Mono track which provide a pure monophonic (1KHz Sine Wave) tone and unmute the master. Now onwards don't dare to touch any parameters of the compressors inserted to those 4 auxiliaries. Now import the audio tracks.

9. At first, re-verify the whole audio editing process (First filter out unwanted frequencies using filters, Balance the sound pressure level of each track with other tracks by inserting a gain tool at each channels' insert for -18dBFS RMS SPL setting, then use pan or width control and apply desired value - high frequencies can be panned more than low frequencies, then check the phase issues by sending both left and right signals to a mono speaker or can be panned the master to left or switch the master buss from stereo to mono; if sounds louder in mono speakers means all the channels' signals are in phase, less level in mono speakers indicates some of the channels' signals are out of phase at certain frequency ranges)

10. The Compressor inserted auxiliaries (Digital, VCA, Tube, Opto, FET) will be routed to the respective groups of

auxiliaries (Front, Middle, Rear, Bass) in series and the groups'auxiliaries' outs need to be routed to master

11. The VariMu subgroup auxiliary can be routed to REAR group and the REAR group can be routed to the Master Channel. In this case all the tracks, that are line sources having sustained sounds, can be routed in series to VariMu Subgroup Auxiliary.

12. The VCA subgroup auxiliary can be routed to MIDDLE group and the MIDDLE group can be routed to the Master Channel. In this case all the tracks, that are line sources having transient sounds, can be routed in series to VCA sub group auxiliary.

13. The Optical subgroup auxiliary can be routed to FRONT group and the FRONT group can be routed to the Master Channel. In this case all the tracks, that are point sources (Lead Instruments) having sustained sounds, can be routed in series to Optical subgroup auxiliary.

14. The Digital subgroup auxiliary can be routed to FRONT group and the FRONT group can be routed to the Master Channel. In this case all the tracks, that are point sources (Lead Instruments) having sustained sounds, can be routed in series to Digital subgroup auxiliary.

15. Front Stereo Aux - Send those channels' signals (transient signals) to Front Stereo Aux which you want to put at the front of your mix. Create an aux and name it as "Front".Put a bus as pre-fader at the send insert of channel strip and set the bus as the front aux input. Use distortion, envelope shaping plugins to get right kind of transient sound according to the tempo at the channel strip if required and use mix knob like a bus send of each signal processing unit. While using harmonic distortion to an instrument, start with high frequency instruments and end with low frequency instruments.

16. Middle Stereo Aux - Send those channels' signals (medium sustained signals) to the Middle Stereo Aux which you want to put at the middle of your mix. Create an aux and name

it as "Middle".Put a bus as pre-fader at the send insert of channel strip and set the bus as the middle aux input. Use distortion, envelope shaping plugins and delay plugin to get right kind of sustain sound according to the tempo at the channel strip if required and use mix knob like a bus send of each signal processing unit. While using harmonic distortion to an instrument, start with high frequency instruments and end with low frequency instruments.

17. Rear Stereo Aux - Send those channels' signals (more sustained signals) to Rear Stereo Aux which you want to put at the rear of your mix. Create an aux and name it as "Rear". Put a bus as pre-fader at the send insert of channel strip and set the bus as the rear aux input. Use distortion, envelope shaping plugins and delay plugin to get right kind of sustain sound according to the tempo at the channel strip if required and use mix knob like a bus send of each signal processing unit. While using harmonic distortion to an instrument, start with high frequency instruments and end with low frequency instruments.

18. Bass Mono Aux - Send those channels' signals (sustained bass frequency signals) to Bass Mono Aux, which you want to put at the front of your mix. Create an aux and name it as "Bass".Put a bus as pre-fader at the send insert of channel strip and set the bus as the front aux input. Use distortion, envelope shaping plugins to get right kind of sustained bass sound according to the tempo at the channel strip if required and use mix knob like a bus send of each signal processing unit. While using harmonic distortion to an instrument, start with high frequency instruments and end with low frequency instruments.

19. For Tonal Compression, you can send the channel's signal to any of the aux (VariMU, Opto, VCA, FET) parallely.e.g.:- A vocal channel's output is going to a VariMu compressor such as Fair Child 660 or Manley VariMU compressor (in series) to which all the backing vocals are routed (in series).

But if you need an extra bite, then from vocal channel we can send a copy (30%) of the audio signal parallely to an FET compressor 1176, 10% of copy of lead vocal can be sent parallely to VCA compressor too.

20. During Series processing, all the values of bus should have a constant value (like consuming a sweet dish)

21. During Parallel processing, all the values of bus should vary as per our need (like the way we consume different variety of dishes during having our lunch)

22. Now create a stereo or 2 mono auxiliaries for a combination of echo, reverb, desired dynamic processor, EQ which can be used for parallel processing from all the lead instruments to the stereo FX auxiliaries or two mono FX auxiliaries which are panned to left & right. The FX auxiliary outputs go to master channel's input. Lead mono Aux - Send those channels' signals (Lead instruments' signals) which you want to put at the centre of your mix. Create an aux & name it as "Lead Mono".Put a bus as pre-fader at the send insert of channel strip and set the bus as the rear aux input to the VariMu Compressor. Use distortion, envelope shaping plugins and delay plugin to get right kind of sustain sound according to the tempo at the channel strip if required and use mix knob like a bus send of each signal processing unit. While using harmonic distortion to an instrument, start with high frequency instruments and end with low frequency instruments.

23. Chorus and Bridge areas are having louder SPL; so at first, mix them by following the above processes (from 1st process to 15th process).Verses carry an average SPL ; so at second, mix the verse areas. Pre-chorus has a transition of softer to louder SPL which provide a clear and transparent information about dynamic range of the song with in less time frame (2 bars to 4 bars); so at third, mix the pre-chorus area. Outro and Chorus may carry louder sound or softer sound; so at fourth, mix the chorus and outro area. Intro used to have very

soft sound; so at last, mix the intro area. If possible, you can automate 1st dimension parameters [filters and equalisers], 2nd dimension parameters [pan potentiometer control] and 3rd dimension parameters [the amount of reverb and echo (delay+reverb) and the threshold level of compressors when the song switches from one section of song to another section of the song (intro to verse, verse to pre-chorus, pre-chorus to chorus, chorus to bridge, bridge to outro)]

Note:

1. Introducing another instrument's sound to the same compressor will change the sweet spot of the compressor; if you do that, then you need to calibrate the parameters of the compression again to achieve the sweet spot (which means - Compressors should breathe according to the tempo)
2. As a Mix Engineer, you need to bring out the feel and excitement of the song by crafting the artists' performances using the knowledge you have and implementing them using available tools.
3. Mix the lead instruments first (Point Sources and Line Sources) which lead the entire song.
4. Then mix the supporting equipments (Point Sources and Line Sources), which complements the lead instruments
5. The other instruments such as fillers and synth pads to glue the whole song at the third (Point Sources and Line Sources)
6. Take a 15 minutes break after working on your mix for 45 minutes. Spend less than 1 minute time to listen and solve a problem or betterment of a sound or musical instrument during mixing process. You should not be obsessed to mix one song for longer period of time (12 Hrs Max per day). Working on multiple mix projects refresh the perception and brings new ideas. If you felt that you are either obsessed or fed up by listening and mixing to the song for a longer time period, then open up another project, work for 5 minutes or

open one of your favourite project or any other artists' song and listen and work on it. After 5 to 10 minutes, open the previous project on which you were working before 5 to 10 minutes

7. To make a sound source closer to you, use Dynamic Based 3-tier mix processes
8. To increase depth content in the song, use Time Based 3-tier mix processes
9. Use 2 volume techniques (monitoring the whole process at a decent 90dB SPL at maximum and also at lower level)
10. Check the phase issues (Absolute, Relative) by listening

2.3.3.6. *Mixing for Immersive Sound Experience*:

For stereophonic sound experience in 180 degree space environment, you always considering yourself as a stationary object where as others as moving objects.

For Immersive sound experience in 360 degree space environment, you always considering yourself as a moving object and also considering other objects as moving object except one of them that you have chosen as stationary for your reference for a certain time period. In this case, your brain always keep searching to select one of the moving objects as stationary one for your reference and switch to that selected object considering as a stationary object. It means, the process of selecting and considering one of the moving objects as stationary, is very much dynamic in nature. Therefore, perception of immersive sound experience of each human being varies.

Dolby Atmos is an immersive sound experience that make you feel like you are the part of the story conveyed by the visuals. Here a new approach is added with the surround sound, known as Beds, that use a concept called Objects. The information about each object's position in a 360 degree view of the environment is called Metadata.

1. Ego-centric Approach: In this case, we do virtual reality(VR) mixing for gaming industries. In this case, the head tracking

feature is added to the VR headsets used by the consumers or to the built-in front camera powered by artificial intelligence chipsets of mobile phone, tablets or computer. Here the consumer is the lead character. The consumption of audio-visual is based on the perception of lead character. The consumer enjoys being the lead character for entertainment. That's why the position of the consumer is dynamic and his/her consideration of objects changes as per his/her preference.

2. Alo-centric Approach: In this case, we mix for Music Video and Film Projects. Here the mix is based on the lead character played by an actor on the screen and the other sounds are mixed around the lead character according to the visuals. The consumer is treated as third party. The consumption of audio-visual is based on the perception of lead character. The consumer enjoys watching the characters for entertainment. That's why the position of the consumer is static.

Basically the Dolby Atmos has two sections or groups called Beds and Objects. The Dynamic Sound Sources(e.g. foley sounds during a fight scene, dialogues of the character), that has informations about pointed direction or position, can be routed to Objects group where as the Static Sound Sources(e.g. background music score) having no directional informations and the Ambient Sounds(e.g. Forest Ambiance, Traffic Ambiance, Street Ambiance, Crowd Ambiance during sports or cultural events, room ambiance... etc.) that doesn't have informations about any direction or position, can be routed to Beds group. In beds group, the Ambient Sound used to be routed towards Ceiling Speakers where as the Music can be routed to Surround Speakers. The Ambient Sound can be treated as a Point Source and can be routed to Objects group if a football field, a cricket ground or a music festival arena has been shot on drone camera far from the sky at much height from the earth's surface. It is all about perception of sound according to the audio visuals. Sound that has directions can be treated as Objects. Sounds that doesn't has directions can be treated as Beds. We do audio signal processing at the master bus for Bed tracks collectively where as we do audio signal processing individually for Object Tracks. The audio signal processing at the master bus won't affect the Object Tracks.

Please remember that mixing in Dolby Atmos is much easier than mixing in mono.

CHAPTER 2.4

SOUND MASTERING

The listeners consume music from different analog platforms (Physical Products such as LP Records, EP Records, Analog Tape Cassette) and digital platforms (Physical Products such as CD, DVD and Broadcasting on radio and television, other digital audio streaming platforms on internet such as Youtube, Spotify, iTunes, Jio Saavn…etc).So for such different platforms, the mastering engineer process a mixed song in different ways to make it audible from a mobile phone speaker to a movie theatre speaker system.

A mastering engineer prepares the mixed audio files for distribution for different platforms and make sure whether all the elements (each instrument played, foley sound, dialogues and lyrics) are audible or noticeable properly on the speaker of each audio device such as a car audio system, a mobile phone speaker, a television speaker, a laptop speaker, headphones, earphones, ceiling speakers in a mall (super market), home theatre speaker system, speaker system of a cinema hall, speaker system of a conference hall …etc.

Note: During mastering a slow tempo song, we use slow attack (longer or more attack time) and slow release (longer or more release time) settings in a compressor so that the sound sources can breathe according to the tempo. During mastering a fast tempo song, we use fast attack (shorter or less attack time) and fast release(shorter or less release time) settings in a compressor so that the sound sources can breathe according to the tempo.

After Mastering Process, the Mastering Engineer transfers the analog sound from analog tape to an LP record or an EP Record to playback and monitor the sound. After approval of quality check, the Mastering Engineer transfer the analog sound from the respective LP/EP Record to many digital audio formats for different digital platforms. Most of skilful Disk Jockeys and good listeners to music, prefer an LP or EP record system for playback the audio because an LP Record System and an EP Record System provide very rich audio quality as compared to the other playback systems available in the market.

Always communicate and keep in touch with the Sound Recordist, Sound Editor and Mix Engineer and document the informations regarding audio equipments used in recording, editing and mixing, places of recording, editing, mixing, process of recording editing and mixing, the problems resolved by Sound Recordist, Sound Editor and Mix Engineer and to be resolved by Mastering Engineer... etc. Import your audio tracks in your work station, rename them, colour code them; then you start your work on mastering.

2.4.1. Stereo Mastering Technique:

1. Check Gain Staging Process and compare your work with one of the mastered tracks from your playlist for your reference or use the mastered track suggested by your client
2. Insert VU meter plugin and analyse the feel of the song and overall level of the song
3. Check the phase issues (Absolute Phase issues and Relative Phase issues) by putting the mixed stereo track in a mono track and pan it to one of the speaker. The overall level should be louder in mono which is a clear sign that left and right signals are in phase
4. Understand the platform for which you are mastering (Youtube, iTunes, Saavn, Theatre, TV, Radio Broadcasting ... etc - Understand different K-System Values).Your work should sound as good as other competitor

5. Use a co-relation meter - Left signal and Right signal are co-related in terms of frequencies, SPL ...etc. The objective is all the signals should be constructive. The negative side of co-relation meter indicates that the mix is not right

6. Use of Phase Cohesion - Check for phase issues

7. If you go for balloon analogy, then first use a limiter (Waves L2 Ultramaximizer - Brickwall Limiter, Logic Pro's Adaptive Limiter, Fairchild 670/660, Vladislav Goncharov's Limiter No6, Maximal 2 by Venomode, Rough Rider) at the end of the insert to bring out the average volume. The setting of this limiter is as follows: Out Ceiling = -0.3dB (-0.2dB for big band or orchestra), Over Sampling = Put it on for not to loose any samples, Over all gain reduction = -6dB, set link control on, set threshold level for 6dB gain reduction and monitor that whether the gain reduction happens according to tempo or not

   Before using any audio signal processor, if you find any aural differences between left and right signals of a stereo track, then use your preferred multiple mono audio signal processor or unlink the stereo signal processor to process left and right signals separately or split the stereo audio file to import in 2 mono tracks for processing left and right signals individually

8. If required, use a compressor (API 2500, Neve 33609/C, Tokyo Dawn Labs' TDR Kotelnikov, Shadow Hills Mastering Compressor)

9. If required, use a harmonic distortion and after that MS (Mid-Side or Lateral-Vertical) type EQ (REDD 17 and 37-51 Tube EQ, Shatter Galass Audio Lab's Code Red Free, Fabfilter EQ, Waves HEQ) and MS type Compressor (Fairchild 670, Vladislav Goncharov's Molot).Crossover frequencies of all consumer level used to be 80Hz and 120Hz. On sides cut below 80Hz using HPF with Baxandal Curve (6dB or 12 dB per octave). We can increase 0.5 dB of Chorus and Bridge sections of Side channels using Mid-Side processing through Automation. For hiphop and pop song, cut the HF using shelving EQ by 1 or 2dB which is not recommended for Indian percussion instruments such as

tabla, dholak …etc. On low frequencies, cut off below 30 Hz and boost above 75Hz. Cross check whether the high frequencies are loud or fine using Low Cut Filter (High Pass Filter) at 250Hz and 500Hz. Cut the unwanted frequencies from mids and highs. Or in another way, increase lower mid, cut high frequencies on sides as per required and increase LF, HF and cut MF resonance bell curves on mid. Increase the volume of sides more than mid for more wideness in this mid-side techniques. Always listen what changes you are making on EQ through a compressor if you are using EQ before Compressor, then you can identify the problematic frequencies very easily because the speaker cone is moving efficiently according to the tempo as per you settings in the compressor.

10. If there is no head room, then use a little reverb.
11. As per the audio signal chain first slot onwards from left to right, Co-Relation Meter -> Harmonic Distortion -> EQ (MS Type) -> VCA Mastering Compressor -> Mastering EQ -> Vacuum Tube based Compressor (for MS Processing) -> Limiter. As per processing, Co-Relation Meter -> Limiter -> Harmonic Distortion -> VCA Mastering Compressor -> Mastering EQ -> Vacuum Tube based Compressor (for MS Processing) -> EQ (MS Type)
12. Insert proper silence at start and end of the audio
13. Then export the sound with in the required formats (based on 1 bit DSD, PCM with 32 bit Bitdepth and 384 KHz Sample Rate) for each platform as per request by the client
14. After mastering open all mastering plugins and make a snapshot or screenshot for your reference
15. Have as many backups as possible (with maintaining privacy because before getting audio materials you have signed an NDA form - Non Disclosure Agreement form) of your session files and save them also on online storage location such as google drive, iCloud …etc
16. Get an ISRC code and embedded that code with the mastered audio